MY RICH UNCLE

An Informal Guide
to Maximizing Your Enlistment

A.J. Kehl

Savas Beatie
California

Library of Congress Cataloging-in-Publication Data

Names: Kehl, A. J., author.
Title: My Rich Uncle: An Informal Guide to Maximizing Your Enlistment in the United States Air Force / by A. J. Kehl.
Other titles: Informal Guide to Maximizing your Enlistment in the United States Air Force
Description: First edition. | El Dorado Hills, California: Savas Beatie, [2019] | Includes bibliographical references.
Identifiers: LCCN 2019008882| ISBN 9781611214673 (pbk : alk. paper) | ISBN 9781611214680 (ebk)
Subjects: LCSH: United States. Air Force–Officers–Handbooks, manuals, etc. | United States. Air Force—Military life. | United States. Air Force-—Recruitment, enlistment, etc.
Classification: LCC UG633.K418 2019 | DDC 358.40023/73—dc23
LC record available at https://lccn.loc.gov/2019008882

First Edition, First Printing

Savas Beatie
989 Governor Drive, Suite 102
El Dorado Hills, CA 95762
916-941-6896 / sales@savasbeatie.com / www.savasbeatie.com

Our titles are available at special discount rates for bulk purchases in the United States. Contact us for more information.

Proudly published, printed, and warehoused in the United States of America.

This book is dedicated to all those who serve
in the enlisted forces. Civilians will never understand.

Table of Contents

Preface

The hard part is over.

You spent a few of your hard-earned dollars and took a chance on a book by some guy with a MacBook and a desire to share valuable information. Well, I thank you and I'm confident it will be money well spent. I render this as true because I spent months gathering thoughts and ideas from many of the world's most knowledgeable enlisted members. Countless hours have been spent preparing this hodgepodge of a guide. In the end, a manual of sorts has been established.

My Rich Uncle is not about taking for granted the immense benefits the military offers or about finding loopholes that breach character, but rather it is about maximizing the services offered and reaping the often intangible rewards of this chapter in your life. This book is written so anyone can pick it up and take something away. Whether you are thinking of joining, you're already a member, or you're a veteran looking for more information to bestow upon the younger generation, *My Rich Uncle* is for you.

We begin with, well, the beginning. The journey ahead is interesting to say the least. Life-altering events, one after another, lead you to build a network around yourself. This community spreads like wildfire across the globe and has an enormous return on investment. Moving forward, you'll learn ways to effectively survive the new universe around you. Your personal and professional lives will never be the same, and managing your enlisted life is paramount. I will guide you through all the variables that will inevitably come your way so you can develop daily, breeding success.

Becoming whole and finding yourself is the greatest benefit of the military, but there are thousands of other reasons why this life, the military life, is abound with benefits and advantages that common civilians will never experience. You will quickly see that as your life moves forward, learning, adapting, and traveling. Those you grew up with (at least the majority of them) will be seemingly standing still as time passes them by. You'll eagerly go home to visit friends and family only to find they are still bagging groceries at the local Albertson's or still working for their dad at the town's only auto shop. This isn't a bad thing by any means, but your eyes will widen as you realize what you are doing is important and unique. How unique? Well, so unique that only 1 percent of Americans embark on this journey. I would say that is pretty unique!

As of this writing, I have been in the military for a little over 15 years. In that time, I have been to 67 countries, held ten different duty titles, been a part of four wartime deployments, and met extraordinary people who have shaped who I am as a person and given me opportunities I would have never been fortunate to have had I not joined the Air Force.

These experiences and gathering of knowledge are laid out throughout this book with special highlights called "MRU Tips" just for you. Of course, MRU stands for "My Rich Uncle." These tips can range from enlisted life advice to tips on maximizing your Government Travel Charge Card benefits.

The Air Force is a true blessing, and for those of you who are thinking of joining, you won't regret it. Even if you only stay long enough to get out of mom's house, it will be worth your investment of time. If you are currently serving and picked up this book out of curiosity, use it however you like. Pull random things out that can lift you higher in your pursuit of enlisted success. I tried to keep it as real as possible and hope you appreciate that as you flip through the content. Finally, for those of you who have served in the past and found your way to this collection of craziness, I hope you find some nostalgic moments and the words bring back old memories. If you haven't already, you will see that the Air Force has probably changed since your day. One day I will be in your shoes, reading the *Air Force*

Times, asking myself why the military keeps changing when things were so awesome in my day. Who knows? All I know is this book is written for everyone, and if you are able to get even one thing out of it, it is all worth it.

If you are looking for a book that reads like the well-written articles by your installation PA office, you picked up the wrong book. This won't have sections on core values, manpower and organization, or customs and courtesies. These things are implied and not my intent. Instead, you have your mitts on something I wish was handed to me as a young senior airman. Something raw and real that can be swiftly applied to get to the next level. But this isn't an airman's guide. It is a collection of thoughts, ideas, and solutions. If you read it and apply some of these tips to your enlisted life, I believe you will be on your way to cooking up success. With all that said, there are also some things in here I don't back 100 percent. In a later chapter, I speak about outsourcing and what you can do. Although that is awesome, I am not recommending it, just letting you know it exists. Take what you wish. Brain dump what you think is not value added. I'm just grateful for the opportunity to write this book and hope you enjoy reading it as much as I enjoyed writing it.

AJ Kehl

Acknowledgments

Special thanks to my mom and dad for being super cool.

Many people along the way helped me with this project. If you are not listed here, my apologies. You know who you are, and know that I am thankful. The following were a part of this project or have been influential in my life:

CMSAF Kaleth Wright; CMSgt (Ret.) Juan Lewis; CMSgt Jennifer Brembah; CMSgt (Ret.) Christopher Mohr; Chief Richard Henderson; Chief Matthew Hitchcock; CMSgt Ryan Strub; CMSgt Edwin Ludwigsen; CMSgt Timothy Randolph; Chief Paul Erickson; Jason Kidd; Matthew McNabb; Alex Mace; Kristal Crozier; Manual Makalena; Alexa; Aaron Kehl, Adam Kehl, David Kehl Jr., and Maria Kehl. And my son, C.J.

I would also like to thank my publisher, Savas Beatie, and everyone there for having the faith to publish my book, and for the support they have shown me.

Chapter 1

Beginning Your Journey

Recruiters Don't Lie—They Fib

Never in a million years did I think I would end up at a recruiter. I know I can't be the only one who, when asked, "Why did you join?" has the shrugging shoulder response. Truly, I have no idea, but I'm glad I did! Since I'm from Southern California, it is a given that I smoked pot, so going to the recruiter felt like I was walking into the pot police lion's den. Luckily, my recruiter was pretty awesome and helped me through the process. Of the entire approach leading to MEPS (military entrance processing station, i.e., that place you go to get indoctrinated), my most vivid memory is the moment my recruiter stopped me from being a cop. I was this close (imagine I'm putting my fingers really close together) to being a cop and most likely hating life while I checked ID's at the gate. That's just me though. Our defenders are awesome people and often have to do the dirty work to keep us safe. Hell, some even enjoy proudly standing at the gate and ensuring our installation is guarded from bad people. I can admire that.

Recently, I scoured the Internet for some statistics on recruiters and came across an entertaining piece on them and the lies they tell. I believe the author is genuine, because he prefaced the article with letting his readers know his giant pet peeve is when people lie to recruiters to get into the military. So it goes both ways. It is fascinating that, to get back to your primary job, you need to be a great recruiter, and much of this is based on ensuring you have a blemish-free record. In other words, you have to make your goals. This causes some natural human tendencies to do whatever it takes to get the applicant to MEPS.

There was an ABC special not long ago where students with hidden cameras went to a recruiter, and it was clear the fibbing was rampant. I feel like once a recruiter tells you something like, "Your chances of being deployed to Iraq or Afghanistan are slim to none," you know they don't put too much emphasis on the whole "tell the truth" thing.

Some of the bigger lies I want to share aren't to scare those of you thinking about joining, but rather to keep your spidey senses up and running throughout your experience. Here are a few things recruiters may say that simply aren't true:

- "Once on the delayed entry program, you cannot quit." Uh, yeah you can. Until you actually go on active duty, you can change your mind.
- "If you don't like the military, you can simply quit." This may seem far-fetched, but some recruiters actually say this. Once you are in, you can't just quit, hence the contract.
- "Your chances of getting the assignment you want are really high." LMAO! The needs of the service come way before your needs. With that said, once you are in, especially on a remote or overseas tour, your chances go way up. I put all West Coast US and was sent to Germany. Didn't sound like they really had a need in California at the time.

There are plenty more examples, but I like to jump around. These things are actually said, so be sure you do your own research and don't just accept what the recruiter says at face value. To be honest, the majority of recruiters are hardworking men and women trying to do their job well and support their family. Their ethics are usually in good order, but members unfortunately need to be aware, because lying hasn't yet been eradicated from the earth.

MRU Tip

If you find yourself lied to or feel your recruiter is being unethical, here is a place you can contact: Inspector General, Air Force Recruiting Service, HQ AFRS/CVI, Randolph AFB, TX 78150. Email: aetcigq@us.af.mil.

Q&A with a Former Air Force Recruiter

My friend and colleague Bob spent four years as a recruiter in the Northeastern US. He is one of those guys who will tell it to you straight, regardless of what is being communicated. I knew he was the guy to answer some questions we all may have.

1. Is it true recruiters have to meet a quota?

Yes. There is a quota or goal that comes down each month for the market of your zone (where you recruit out of). They mainly target high school graduates. The nature of your goal really depends on the market you are in and the opportunity within it. Not meeting your goal is clearly not a good thing. Supervisors can place you on mandatory overtime if you suck. If you suck for consecutive months, they move to the next level. Basically, a team will come in and evaluate the data and figure out why you can't make your goal. For me, quotas were between one and four per month. This doesn't seem like too much, but people wouldn't qualify because of things like tattoos, matching a job, credit scores, etc.

2. Have you ever seen or heard about recruiters lying to ensure they enlist someone?

You hear about it from recruits all the time. As you dig deeper, 90 percent of the time, it was some sort of misunderstanding. In recruiting school, there is a joke that says, "Recruiters don't lie; recruits just don't ask the right questions." A lot of it is the fact that recruiters don't know the ins and outs of each particular job in the Air Force. All we can do is our best based on our own experience and knowledge. Just like anything else that is competitive, I'm sure people were lying to get ahead.

3. What are the perks of being a recruiter?

Special duty assignment pay was an extra $450 a month, and you were basically your own boss. The nearest recruiter was 45 minutes away, and my boss was more than an hour away. This made the deal pretty sweet. As long as you met your goal, you could pretty much set your own schedule! We could use our GTC for up to $75 a month on things like applicant meals, but there were too many strings attached to make it a big perk.

4. What tricks do recruiters use to get someone on the hook?

Not so much tricks, but we go through more of a sales course than a traditional technical school. The tactics we use could be perceived as sales tricks, but it's really all about alleviating people's concerns. For instance, say someone says they don't want to go in the Air Force because they will be away from the family. We would tell them about how they also mentioned how they wanted to see the world and how they would have time to see their family due to the fact you get 30 days of annual leave. Again, just taking their concern and trumping it with some of the cool stuff.

5. As a former recruiter, would you trust what a recruiter says?

Yes, but between Facebook and Google, there is almost nothing you can't find out. It isn't like the old days when you just trusted whatever the recruiter said. I highly advise you to validate what they are saying. I would be careful to do this and the old "trust but verify" routine.

Don't Miss the Starting Gun

> *"How much I missed, simply because I was afraid of missing it."*
> — Paulo Coelho

Joining the military, or even just leaving home to pursue something that interests you, is a gigantic milestone in your life, and preparedness is contrary to reason. This is because the twists in your stomach that occur when you leave everything you have ever known is unsettling in its own way. This tremendous step forward in your life will require you to be on your own, out into the great unknown. But what a ride it will be! It all starts with having the courage to seek growth.

We all want a different outcome and yet most of us don't want any change in our lives. Change brings about uncertainty, and uncertainty equals discomfort, and discomfort sucks. But when we learn to enjoy the process of change, when we choose to look at uncertainty as life's potpourri, then we get to reap the rewards of change.

That is how we grow.

For this section, I will discuss this journey through the lens of my experiences, along with many of my peers, to lay a worthy foundation so traction can occur. The goal is to get you started on the path to enlistment and life success right away. Here's the thing, Pink Floyd got it right in what became one of the greatest songs of all time. It's called "Time." To this day, this song resonates with me on a deeper level. It talks about how so many are just waiting for someone to show them the way and then all of a sudden, ten years have passed by and you realize you missed the starting gun for life. Point being, you just have to go for it and do it when you are young and hungry to take on life itself.

This song is so true. Time is finite and scarce. When that day comes, and ten years has passed you by, what can you say you did? Did you make something of yourself? Did you get a chance to see the world? Did you take a chance and wander into the unknown? I'm not saying that staying in your hometown and making a living is bad. Hell, we all need to make a living. But what if I told you that you could easily be part of that small number of people who actually venture off, see the world, make friends in countless countries, and develop in a way that cannot be compared to anything else on this planet? Would you believe me if I said that route is the US military? Well, it is. So don't miss the starting gun.

During the duration of this guide, I will show you how to maximize your enlistment to the fullest. You will know right out of the gate what is and isn't important, along with the perfect recipe as to how we can make some scrumptious lemonade from all of life's lemons! If you're already in the service, *perfect*! It is never too late to learn about what is right in front of you. The best part is that you probably can relate to most of the following content because there are so many universal truths. For example, the world of TDYs and how freaking awesome they can be. This guide is not merely a source for sound advice and tips, it is a book to throw in your drawer at the office, take out every once in a while, and read a little something to keep you moving in the right direction. Lastly, if you have served in the armed forces in any capacity, I believe you will appreciate some of the leadership and Veterans Affairs sections, along with the famous military intelligence (and other oxymorons) chapter, which was a unique venture to say the least. More than 100 service members provided some humor that will never get old! You see, this is where it all starts. You took the plunge and are ready to learn about that rich relative of yours and all the ways he can help you out. Are you ready? Let's go!

Basic Training

> *"You're five-foot-nine. I didn't know they stacked shit that high."*
> — Gunnery Sgt. Hartman (from the movie "Full Metal Jacket")

Okay, it's not like that. Well, it is if you chose a service besides the Air Force (sorry guys). I spoke with a few drill sergeants with the Marine Corps and Army, and they are in-line with Stanley Kubrick's masterpiece. The Marines go to Perris Island for a 12-week suck fest. More than 20,000 Marines leave the recruit depot every year, and although I respect those men and women, I wouldn't want to be a part of that.

Basic training is something all services do slightly different, but the basic premise is the same: weed out the weak and get people processed into the real military. The Air Force undoubtedly has the easiest ride, but even so, it isn't fun.

Basic training is not difficult. If you are thinking of joining the Air Force but afraid of basic, don't be. It is cake. The point of it is to pay attention to the details. Meaning, do what you are told exactly how you are told. If you have been through Air Force basic training, you know what I'm talking about, and if you come back with "But mine was different, it was really hard," I would have to call you out for lying. Only those who graduated in 2004 or earlier have a leg to stand on when it comes to a difficult experience. This is because those good ole days were before the huge BMT scandal that caused the gnarliest knee-jerk reaction we the people have ever seen. Seemingly overnight, the Air Force had a tectonic shift, and out came stricter rules, stress cards, and Developmental Special Duties (DSDs).

Without boring us all about basic training, please know that the real Air Force is nothing like it. It is simply a tool to get you to conform to this way of life and weed out those who can't meet basic standards. You have nothing to worry about. What is important is that you keep your head down and try to enjoy the experience, as basic training is more of a glorified in-processing camp than anything else. But let's talk about more important stuff, like building relationships. Keep reading to find out about how critical it is to creating your network.

Your Network Is Your Net Worth

> *"If you want to go fast, go alone. If you want to go far,*
> *go with" others."* — African Proverb

Remember, like-minded individuals from whom we can learn will create the lasting impressions we desire. This is critical as you go through life. It's not who you know—it's who knows *you*.

If I were to ask the successful people I know around the Air Force what the top three keys to their success would be, I'm confident networking would make the list. This is because there is tangible value to creating a solid network around you. My first mentor in the Air Force, back when I had two stripes and a desire to develop, said, "If you want to go somewhere, it is best to find someone who has already been there." In hindsight, this seems like common sense! Why would we try to dig a tunnel when the road is already paved? There are so Figure 1.1 many people who have made it to the top of the enlisted ladder; you will have no trouble finding a mentor to reach down and guide you up. On the AF Portal, there is a mentoring thing you can do where you attach yourself to a mentor who has been there and done that. This mentor can be in your career field or someone who just knows how this all works.

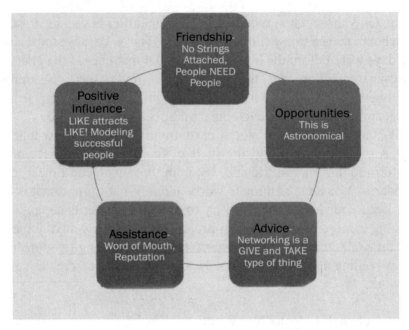

Figure 1.1 *Circle* of Networking Life

Let's sum it all up in one sentence: "Networking has delivered more return on investment than any other tool in my business." By my business, I mean, as an airman, a firefighter, and a glorified business consultant. The key point to remember when you are trying to build up your network within the Air Force is to understand that true, meaningful relationships take time. Okay, sometimes things just click, and boom! You have a legitimate friend and contact. But most of the time you need to add value to that person and have multiple encounters for them to truly be in your inner circle. Going out there with a "What's in it for me?" attitude won't get you very far. Networking is about adding value to others without expectations. In fact, quid pro quo shouldn't even be on your radar. As seen in Figure 1.1, there are so many benefits to networking. The circle of networking life is a lot like "The Lion King," but for networking, *not* Simba.

I think of myself as one who connects people and is connected. My network in the community is linked to many of the opportunities I have been fortunate to receive as well as the successful outcomes that came with them. The funny thing is that many people I know don't want to get hooked up with something because they want to do it themselves. Although I will throw a dash of respect at that, I feel it is a little naive. I don't know anyone who hasn't been helped by their network to land a position, meet the right people, or been covered in order to get something done. We all need help, and it should be welcomed and reciprocated.

Being a connector means you are deliberate. You resonate with people by being genuine and keeping it real. At the end of the day, this is a small Air Force, and burning bridges with someone can have dramatic third- and fourth-order effects. I don't recommend it. There are three ways you can become a connector and build bridges in your expanding network:

- Contact two Facebook friends every day. The typical message that frequently comes your way is from a friend who asks how you are doing, but they really need something from you. We all can relate to this. Want to create impact? Contact two Facebook friends a day just to say hi. Don't ask for anything. Just say hello. Be genuine. Make it clear you are simply seeing how they are doing and reminding them you are available to them at anytime. This powerful move will pay true dividends in many ways.

- Email two professional contacts a week. As with the Facebook initiative, it is important to reach out to people via your work email. Offer them something tangible, like something you recently read or information you've received that you believe may be valuable to them as well. A few of my mentors randomly send me stuff, and I always appreciate it. They don't ask for anything. They are just giving something. You can too.

- Capitalize on your LinkedIn profile. Building a network isn't difficult, but it needs to be enduring. We will all take off this uniform at some point, and your external network is still going to be important to you. Meet an interesting person at the airport? Get their info. Building your profile through sites such as LinkedIn keeps you in touch with professionals and allows them to see your growth. Admittedly, I only make monthly updates; nonetheless, I have experienced so much positivity from these contacts that I know it's worth it. Take some time and build yours. You won't regret it.

Regs You Need to Know

"Simple, clear purpose, and principles give rise to complex intelligent behavior. Complex rules and regulations give rise to simple stupid behavior." — Dee Hock, former CEO of Visa

Anyone who has spent more than two days in the Air Force knows we are governed by regulations. Like a dark cloud that follows us, raining on our parade, regulations are everywhere. There seems to be an Air Force instruction (AFI) for everything, from how you wear your hat, to what you should be thinking at any given time. It is truly endless.

Since there are so many, it is a little daunting to try to figure out which ones you actually need to know, but it is knowing which ones are important and reading those specific regulations that will set you apart from those who don't. Over the course of my career I have realized that something as simple as reading the regulations that govern us makes you smarter than Stephen Hawking. Well, not really, but you'll have a leg up if you read the ones that impact you and those around you. After reading countless AFIs and nodding off into oblivion through most of them, I have a nice list that will help you shorten the time it takes to be a genius. Here are some regulations that, if understood, can set you up for success in the Air Force:

- *36-2110 Assignments:* Want to take control of your path? This one is super important.
- *36-3003 Leave Program:* The big kahuna right here. Find out what you can take as free days and also find out those Joint Travel Regulations (JTR) gifts that keep on giving.
- *36-2903 Dress and Appearance:* Button that freaking pocket! If you don't want to be called out by the uniform police, you will want to know this reg.

- *36-2406 Enlisted Evaluation System:* You can't get promoted if you don't know how. You can't help others understand how things work with performance reports without completely discerning this.

- *36-2618 Enlisted Force Structure:* The little brown book is the road map that doesn't get replaced by that sweet GPS. You need to know your responsibilities to thrive.

MRU Tip
The 36 Series has everything to do with personnel.

- *1-1:* This is the bread and butter right here. This is Air Force culture, otherwise known as the little blue book.

- *36-2805 Special Trophies and Awards:* In the section "Why Awards Do matter," I will lay out why you will want to know what awards are out there, which you are eligible for, and which are actually worth your time.

- *AFH 33-337 The Tongue and Quill:* I cannot stand how rigid some things are for all the nonners out there, but I do understand why attention to detail is important, and this handbook is one of the few that will help you, whether you are actually in the Air Force or not. Need to write a Memorandum for Record (MFR)? Look here first.

- *AFI 35-101 Public Affairs Policies and Procedures:* Even if you are doing amazing things, no one really knows unless it comes out of the shadows. Public Affairs (PA) offers everything you need for a good story, some photos, or even a full-scale video production. I could write a chapter on how important it is to know your PA folks and what services they can provide. Many of my successes and those I look up to were attributed to PA helping to get the word out. As you read this, think about something awesome you are doing and ask yourself why PA hasn't done a story on it.

- *AFI 65-601 Budget Guidance and Procedures:* You want to get to the next level? Understand the money. This cannot be overstated. Even if you aren't a Government Purchase Card holder, if you are a noncommissioned officer (NCO), you should have a basic understanding of how the money works. Don't just go around saying, "Oh, yeah, that's a different pot of money" to your peers and subordinates. Too many people do that without knowing what they are saying and it's annoying. Dig in and read. You will be surprised how much knowledge is in this regulation that you can apply to further the progress of your unit.

Last but not least, know any instruction, policy, operating instruction, or guide that has to do with your job! Dive into your Career Field Education Training Plan (CFETP) and find out what your core documents are. Simply reading and understanding these will put you in a new category. The real shame is that your peers are not doing this! Despite the signatures pencil-whipped in their Air Force Training Record (AFTR), they are not taking the time to know their instructions and regulations. Now that's an opportunity to maximize your enlistment!

Chapter 2

The Secret to Survival

A Beginner's Guide to Wrecking Your Personal Life

Your Personal Life Is Not Safe!

If there is one thing I could caution you to about the military, it is that your personal life is not safe. Things may be going great for you, but what about, you know, your significant other. You see, the military is unique in many ways. One of them is the fact that it tears you away from the people you love. Whether it's because you are deployed or because you are due to PCS (permanent chance of station), it will eat you alive. The civilian world cannot fully understand what it is like to be in a position where, in the case of a deployment, your love has to take a little business trip for a while (like six months to a year). This may not seem like an enormous deal, but it is. It is huge. So many things happen during that time, and I will do my best to explain later in this chapter, but first, I want to give you a snapshot of one of my life lessons, brought to you, in part, by a homicidal maniac, namely, the military.

Do not judge me while you read through this example. I understand the common denominator is, well, me. But that doesn't mean there weren't other influences. If you do judge, I honestly can't blame you.

I was a high school basketball player, so I naturally had to date either a cheerleader or a dance team girl. I chose the latter due to the fact most of the cheerleaders were pregnant. My dance team girl was cute. Nice body, loved my lame jokes, and a smile to kill. Oh, and she was a total nutcase! This girl was clearly crazy, but for whatever reason, at the ripe age of 18, I felt I could help her. So I stayed with her through basic training.

When you are 18, you don't know what the hell you are doing. This is true in so many ways. And this is how it goes:

"You are too young. You don't know what you are doing."
"Yes I do! I love her!"
"I know you do, but you are too young to see the bigger picture."
"Whatever. I'm an adult and I know my heart."

You know what I'm talking about, don't you? It's truth in its purest form. But do we listen? Nope. Instead, we follow our misled, often delusional heart.

Technical school at the Louis F. Garland Fire Academy was coming to an end, and it was time to see where I would be headed. During the portion of basic where you get to fill out your dream sheet, I put down, in order, the following places I wanted to be stationed:

Arizona
California
Either Arizona or California

When I found the assignment sheet hanging on the wall, I looked for my name. Sliding my finger across I noticed neither California nor Arizona as my destination. What the hell is Ramstein!? They sent me to Germany! I was so pissed. Germany? I clearly said I wanted to stay on the West Coast!

This is where my personal life began its roller-coaster ride.

In the military, you are often put into precarious situations where your logical reasoning takes a back seat to dumbass reasoning. I can't tell you how many people I know got married because they were under pressure due to a PCS (permanent chance of station) and ended up marrying someone they otherwise shouldn't have. This is wrong for many reasons. Namely, you are supposed to marry the person you want to spend the rest of your life with, not the person who you simply can't let go of. For those of you reading this that have been in this position, you know exactly what I'm talking about. If you are still together and happy, you are a very rare breed indeed! Most often, people end up resenting their partner, and things unravel from there. After two divorces and over a decade of military life, my advice to you is to relax and wait it out. Sure, if she is the one, go for it. No regrets. But if you know in your gut (the place where truth hangs out) that guy or girl isn't the one, *don't do it!* More often than not, your gut will be correct. Use your head, man—I mean your other one!

Joshua Fields of *The Minimalist* wrote an article we all need to be slapped in the face with. He titled it *"Letting Go of Shitty Relationships."* Fields observed, "We often develop relationships out of convenience, without considering the traits necessary to build a successful bond with another person—important traits like unwavering support, shared trust, and loving encouragement." Tell me this isn't the truth! In the military, it seems we develop relationships based on proximity. That is, we get a thing going with someone simply because they are around and not because they truly add value to our lives. They are in your unit, they are at your base (try being single overseas), or they are a schoolmate. What happens is we end up in a relationship with this person and they drain us, not allowing us to reach our potential in life. They take and take from us without giving anything back. This is a barrier to our resilience, and many of us in the armed forces have to deal with this weight on our shoulders. How do we get back to our purpose-driven lives?

The most prolific piece of advice is to end a relationship that cannot be changed. It is tough. It often feels like your stomach is being pitted within, but this is the one thing you owe yourself, and you cannot rise with the enlisted force if you are being dragged down along the way. You are in control. Understand, marriage can be great. Just do it for the right reasons or your personal life will be as disastrous as the *Titanic*.

Okay, let's shift gears on this marriage thing.

Arranged Marriage in the Military

Time and again I see two people inquiring about getting married so they can get more money. I mean, it sounds nice, right? The assumption is, if you get married, you will be mil to mil or even mil to civilian—and then you will be ballin' (that means you will have a lot of money).

This is not true.

The fact is that getting married for the sake of making more money is not only naive but also senseless. This thoughtless attempt at putting more money in your pocket can cost you in the long run in ways that can undermine your ability to maximize your enlistment.

Okay, since I always try to see both sides of the story, let's take a look at the financial perks that lure everyone in.

If you are a single E-1, you live in the dorms and get your meals at the dining facility. Your income is very low, around $18,000 a year. On the flip side, if you are an E-1 and married, you will receive a basic allowance for housing (around $1,200 a month) plus a basic allowance for subsistence (since you no longer eat for free at the chow hall, around $325 a month). If you marry a civilian, your spouse will get medical coverage. Tricare alone would have many people running toward the contract of marriage.

The difference financially is huge.

Although I'm against a contract marriage because of the lack of integrity and your blatant misuse of a beneficial system, it would provide a financial boost in the beginning. You could easily place an ad on Craigslist and land a wannabe wife. Who needs Russian brides!?

Well, I guess we are sold, right? Nope. There is a big *but* (not butt). First, what if the arrangement doesn't work out? Anyone who has gone through a military divorce knows how messed up they can be. Depending on where you are stationed, it may be next to impossible to even know what county to file in. Second, if you have an arranged marriage, you may not actually get to be intimate with the other person. Too bad, because you can't mess around with anyone else. That's called adultery, and the Uniform Code of Military Justice (UCMJ) really doesn't like that (see Article 134 if you don't believe me).

In the end, we want to maximize our enlistment. You simply can't do that if you are risking so much just for a little extra money. What is BAH (basic allowance for housing) and BAS if you are tied up in a legal battle or, worse, in jail for adultery? Don't get me started on the fact that your retirement pension plays a role, as does the possibility of having a child with someone you didn't marry for love.

Always look for ways to leverage your entitlements and benefits. Just stay away from this loophole, because it could cost you more than you make.

The Airman Bucket List*

Airmen must complete these 10 things their first enlistment:

1. **Get a good mentor.** Find one or two NCOs who are sharp and motivating. Stick with them. They will teach you the ropes and transform you into the sharp airman you aspire to be. Make sure your supervisor knows why you joined the Air Force and what you expect to accomplish.

2. **Apply for a passport and travel.** Don't stay in one place your entire enlistment. Get out and see the world. When you take leave, explore the area. Experience another culture. You get 30 days of leave every year, so do something amazing with them.

3. **Take advantage of all Air Force benefits!** For example, Air Force Association (AFA) Scholarships, CLEP test, vocational rehab, and tuition assistance. Either use it or lose it. Try to earn your Community College of the Air Force (CCAF) before the end of your first enlistment.

4. **Get certifications.** If your job offers national certification, get it. A certification will assist with securing your future after the military. It will also make getting a job much easier and make job opportunities less limited.

5. **Make a scrapbook.** Being in the military will always be a big part of your life, just like high school. Keeping photos and mementos of your experiences will make a great story you can share with your children and grandchildren. Every time you get promoted, save a set of your stripes and participate in all ceremonies.

*The Airman's Bucket List was created by CCM Juan Lewis, *The Fired Up Chief*.

6. **Schedule an appointment with an Airman and Family Readiness Financial Counselor!** Get a free one-on-one financial briefing about the Thrift Savings Plan (TSP), deployment investment, the Soldier and Sailor Act, and the Military Saves program. Before you make a huge purchase, consult your family or your supervisor. Don't let debt control you. If you follow these tips, a trip to Hawaii becomes more realistic, doesn't it? You've got to start early stacking paper and making it rain!

7. **Volunteer once a year for the Recruiter Assistance Program!** Wear your uniform home and visit your high school. It is the perfect opportunity to display how proud you are to be in the Air Force and to inspire those who might be uncertain about their future.

8. **Tie up any loose ends with your family.** Some airmen leave home on bad terms. If you do, be the bigger person and make amends. It is a part of life and an even bigger part of growing up. When all is said and done, family is everything. Make sure you communicate with your family, and you will realize your family truly cares about you.

9. **Network.** There are reasons why you meet people in life. There are other airmen out there who have skills you don't have. It is a great way to learn new trades and it's free of charge.

10. **Get involved with the base and your community.** No, I'm not talking about sucking up. I'm referring to giving back to the people who support you. Volunteering for Habitat for Humanity or a food kitchen is a great way to show your appreciation for their support. Nothing pleases the soul better than helping those in need, and nothing touches the heart more than a smile and a simple "Thank you for serving our country."

The NCO Bucket List

The Fired Up Chief, CCM (ret.) Juan Lewis, sets the stage for the NCO corps with this bucket list to follow if you are an NCO. Chief is a one-of-a-kind leader and thousands of people follow his words of wisdom. Take some nuggets as you wish.

1. **Create six goals you will accomplish as a technical sergeant!** Write a list of six goals you will accomplish as a technical sergeant. They can either be professional or personal goals. Keep a copy on your refrigerator, in your office, in your wallet, etc. Share them with the world so others can motivate you to stay focused and on track.

2. **Read leadership books!** To be a successful leader, you must be an avid reader. Leadership books such as One Minute Manager, Who Moved My Cheese, etc., will bolster your ability to lead and inspire heroes.

3. **Write your last will and testament!** Go by the Legal Office and have the experts draft this important document. You can never be too prepared! Make sure you keep it in a safe place.

4. **Write yourself a letter and read it at your retirement ceremony!** Focus your letter on the challenges you faced and defeated, what you consider important, and where you see yourself headed in the next decade. Seal it, keep it in a safe place, and read it when you retire.

5. **Connect with a former teacher or supervisor to express your thanks!** Write a thank-you letter that highlights the things you feel your teacher or supervisor has helped you with or inspired you to do. Keep it brief and factual.

6. **Lead by example!** The quickest way to lose the respect of those around you is to be hypocritical! While this may be one of the hardest things to do, it is a must! For example, if you expect your airmen to score a 90 or above on their PT test, you need to be able

to do the same. If for some reason you cannot score a 90, then make sure they see you working hard toward that 90. If you say lunch is an hour long, don't stroll in 15 to 20 minutes late.

7. **Buy a mess dress!** If you aspire making senior master sergeant, go ahead and purchase a mess dress uniform. It sends a signal you are committed to the Air Force. The sooner you buy one, the cheaper it is. Every time I wear it, I smile and think of the return on my investment.

8. **Engage in a one-on-one meeting with a chief and first sergeant!** Have them explain the expectations of a technical sergeant. What do they demand and need from a technical sergeant? Hopefully, the session is not focused on future promotion; instead, it needs to be centered on the role of technical sergeants, your responsibilities as a technical sergeant, and what you need to do to positively impact your flight, squadron, etc.

9. **Find a mentor inside and outside your career field!** To continue to grow, you will need mentors inside and outside of your career field. If all your mentors look like you, sound like you, and talk like you, you are missing out. Don't expect them to come to you. You need to be proactive and seek them out.

10. **Invite airmen to your house on holidays!** For some of our heroes, it's the first time they have been away from their families over a holiday period. Don't invite. Tell them if they have no plans, they are coming to your house for holiday dinners. While they are at your place, make them call home and talk to their parents.

11. **Know your base history!** Too often, NCOs are assigned to bases and do not have a clue about the base history. For example, when was the base opened? How did the base acquire its name? What are some famous landmarks on the installation?

12. **Live by these maxims!**
   a. Try and fail. Don't fail to try.
   b. Do the right thing instead of the political thing. You are not running for office.
   c. Volunteer to lead or be forced to follow. Either way, the heroes are moving forward.
   d. Heroes don't rise to the occasion, they fall to the level of their training.
   e. Wear your stripes on your sleeves instead of your butt to protect your ass.
   f. To whom much is given, much is expected.

The Master Sergeant Bucket List

The Fired Up Chief, CMSgt (Ret.) Juan Lewis, composed this informative and powerful master sergeant bucket list. If you are about to be a SNCO or you are already, this is for you!

Are you fired up? Are you motivated? Are you full of Pride, Enthusiasm, and Passion (PEP) about your selection to Master Sergeant? I hope so! YOU ARE PART OF HISTORY . . . Forever etched into the Air Force History.

In 10 years, people will remark how you were part of monumental change under the "immature" promotion system.

Along with this advancement come some huge expectations. Therefore, you must provide "return on investments" as the Air Force continues to navigate this turbulent era, which is filled with uncertainty.

You are in the right place, you are at the right time, and for all you NASCAR fans, you are in the right pole position to lead the Air Force.

The Eyes of America are upon you. The Air Force depends on you while Heroes desperately yearn for your unselfish leadership.

You should feel extremely nervous because you will be propelled to new limits. The more the Air Force pushes, the more you will need to elevate your game to reach your fullest potential.

Being a phenomenal SNCO will require you to raise your performance to new levels.

Don't worry or don't be afraid! And remember, it's okay to struggle and it's all right to feel challenged!

Here are some tips to help you adjust and successfully navigate this "exciting" journey:

a. **You are now MSgt!** Don't wait until you sew on the stripe to start performing and doing what's expected of SNCOs! Your EPR will close out with other MSgts' reports, so you need to act like a MSgt and be like a MSgt upon receiving notification of selection.

b. **Create 5 Goals you will Accomplish as MSgt!** Publicize these goals . . . make sure they are personal and professional. Share with your bosses, heroes, and family so you will be held accountable.

c. **Engage in 1/1 Meeting with a "throwback" Chief!** Ask about SNCO institutional expectations. Bring along the discontinued SNCO Creed and SNCO Charge . . . have the Chief explain in great detail the significance of these old documents.

d. **Understand and Support Big Air Force Messages!** You have to understand the big picture and embrace Air Force decisions. Once these decisions are announced, you have to sell and support as your own. Too often, leaders get so wrapped up in their allegiance to the name tag on the right instead of following the guidance of the name tag on the left. This is the "US" Air Force not a "ME" Air Force

e. **Craft a 3 Minute Elevator Speech!** What's Your Message? If you had 3 mins with a command chief, wing commander, general, senator, or president, what would you say? Take advantage of your seat at the table and have your message ready. If senior leaders ask for your opinion, express your thoughts. Don't reveal problems without proposing solutions.

f. **Honor Veterans on Veterans Day and Pay Respect on Memorial Day!** On Veterans Day, make it a point to honor

Veterans. Show your appreciation by marching in parades, visiting hospitals and veteran homes to listen to their stories and shake their hands for paving the trail for you to follow. On Memorial Day, you should head out to cemeteries to show your respect. Find someone who shares your last name and honor their gravesite with flowers or a memento.

g. **Embrace the Joint Fight!** Welcome the value of having Soldiers, Sailors, Airmen and Marines in your unit and on your installation. The military is headed towards a joint team. You've got to understand and learn the ranks and culture of your sister services. What are the equivalent ranks of a MSgt in the Army, Navy, and Marines? How do you address them? What is their authority?

h. **Know your Airmen & expose them to my other Bucket Lists!** You need to know why they joined, where they are from, where they live, what type of car they drive, who they have car insurance with, what they are doing with their money, and what their goals are. Your ear needs to be to the ground, you need to be aware of what's going on in their lives and if you smell something is wrong, you need to confront it right away. Leaders sniff out problems and help their Airmen solve them

i. **Uphold, Preserve and Sustain military traditions!** The future of the Air Force is in the palm of your hand—recognize it and accept it. Make it a habit to attend Retreats, Dining-In/Out (and know the difference), Air Force Balls, SNCO & Chief Induction Ceremonies, etc. and encourage your Airmen to attend with you.

j. **Purchase new uniforms!** Don't sew new stripes on old faded uniforms. Pass along your old stripes to Heroes to encourage them to follow in your footsteps.

k. **Never stop improving!** Great leaders are constantly learning, stretching themselves, and always trying to improve themselves. Enhance your communication skills! Join Toastmasters and participate in writing seminars. Attend motivational seminars (getmotivated.com), and read motivational and leadership books.

l. **Make the hard call!** Quit pushing tough decisions to your bosses! Too many SNCOs compromise their integrity by endorsing wrong decisions. Lead to be respected instead of being liked!

m. **Update your functional badge!** This is the most neglected item. MSgts who skip this transition point send negative signals such as that they lack proper mentorship.

n. **Learn how to delegate!** The more you delegate, the more you will accomplish. Instead of being in charge of one project, you will be expected to lead multiple assignments. Just remember, delegate authority but retain responsibility.

o. **Write gratitude letters to teachers or supervisors!** Let them know how they made an impact in your life. Don't just mail it; read it in person if you can.

p. **Increase your Thrift Saving Plan!** Make an appointment with a financial planner. Don't just think about your future, start seriously shaping it.

q. **Write letters to your senators & congressmen!** Express your thanks or displeasures about how military quality of life is being positively or negatively impacted. With drastic budget reductions, your voices and concerns need to be heard loud and clear.

r. **We Are All Recruiters (WEAR) Program!** Visit your old high school in uniform. Participate in the WEAR program and recruit someone from your neighborhood to join the military. The military is a fabulous organization and a great venue for people to receive opportunities that will change their lives.

s. **Take Care of Your Airmen and Stick Your Neck on the Line!** You are not their friend . . . you are their leader! Establish the right environment, standards, and expectations, which need to be crystal clear. It's not what you say, it's what you do, and it's all about how you make them feel. You have to show them you truly CARE!!!! Get involved with them, get to know them personally, talk to their family, and let them know you have their back. This is not a one mistake Air Force . . . if they mess up and you feel like they deserve a second chance, don't be a wimp, follow your heart and stick your neck on the line . . . who cares if you get burnt? Your Heroes will truly appreciate the support.

Congrats again, Heroes! I am so proud of you and I expect you to be even prouder about your promotion. You are forever etched into Air Force History. Keep elevating your PEP as you guide the Air Force into the future.

If It's Personal, It's Personnel

Keeping an eye on your personal records is very important when it comes to your career. When you look at virtual Military Personnel Flight (vMPF), you will either find accurate data or a few errors that spark your interest. If you find any errors in your duty history, take a look at the instructions on how to get it fixed via vMPF. Your MPS no longer updates your past duty history, only current duty titles.

Also, your office symbol and duty phone change on a regular basis, making it hard for the Military Personnel Section (MPS) to keep up. The Air Force Personnel Center (AFPC) allows you to update your Defense Switched Network (DSN) line and office symbol yourself via vMPF as well.

The Enlisted Evaluation System

"Evaluation by others is not a guide for me." — Bruce Lee

If one thing is unavoidable, it is your evaluation performance report (EPR). The dreaded EPR seemingly defines who you are (it doesn't really). If you have been around the military for more than four or five years, you know that when people think of the EPR, the term that deafens their eardrums is inflated. "Oh, you remember, Joe over there is a badass. He dominates at work, volunteers in the community, and also has a 4.0 GPA." "John is okay. He comes to work, doesn't mess up really. I mean, he did AADD one time, and I believe he just took a CLEP right before this EPR closeout—let's give them both a 5. What the hell!"

This has been the story for years. We all started at the exact same place (over 85 percent according to AFPC), and it was simply a matter of testing as to who gets promoted. I remember being constantly upset that this was the only way to get promoted. Like many others, I hated the lack of distinction between the great and the subpar. But that's the way it was, until 2015 when things got real. The Air Force decided to enforce quotas for the top tier, and has that caused a stir! In short, 5 percent get the top rating, which is worth 250 points, and then 10 percent get the next best rating, which is worth 220 points. After that, a 3 is only worth 200 points. You quickly get the idea those points matter, and there is now a much different starting line! I love it! When you have only one or two tests that are worth 100 points each, that separation starts to actually mean something. This *hopefully* will promote the right people. But the issue still remains though: people. We the people (the supervisors in particular) will find a way to inflate the crap out of this system too. Below is a little piece from a blog I wrote on how we can deflate this balloon that keeps filling up.

Deflating EPR Inflation

In an EPR system long ago, in an Air Force not so far away, we had an inflated EPR system that gave mediocre Airman the same starting line as the superior performers. The sensational inflation diluted true ratings to the point where if you didn't know the person personally, you would have no clue if they were worth the money the taxpayer pays.

Moving forward, we have now been told that if we can't give fair assessments, the Air Force will drop the mic after forcefully initiating quotas. Yep, that Air Force is here and it's here to stay. We can complain all we want and scream from the brown rooftops, "the system sucked," but it wasn't the system; it was *us*. We allowed the inflation because we couldn't call the baby ugly. Now, here we are, in what I believe is a more effective system that, if nothing else, shows differentiation between the on-par and double eagle.

How do we make sure this too doesn't become overinflated? Well, that's a tough question to answer if we haven't effectively changed our attitudes towards ratings. We all want "our guy" to be well represented, but I think it is fair to say that our guy isn't always the best when he is put up against the rest in the squadron. The key issue at this point (in my opinion), is that someone can be the very best in their flight . . . the #1 Superstar! *and still* not get that Promote Now or Must Promote. What a heartbreaker.

It is critically important that we rank the members against their peers. A solid way to do this is to get all the raters in a room and hash it out. Typically, we all know who the go-to players are. The Additional Rater is in quite a pickle at times because he goes down to the Squadron and sees the competition. Then, he comes back to that Rater and is like, "Hey, man, your dude probably isn't a 5." The Rater can hold strong at that point, but at what cost? First-world problems!

One final note—If you rate someone a 2, it doesn't always have to be a referral EPR. Some people are just 2s, man! In the end, this new EPR rating system has advantages and disadvantages, just like everything else. We can maximize its effectiveness by ensuring we are only pushing forward those that have credibility and deserve to be promoted. One advantage is the quotas and one disadvantage is that the middle of the road, or what we used to call a 3, is a gigantic holding tank and it is tough to distinguish those stuck in it.

As you can see, we have a long road ahead and the only way to make this new process work is to accurately assess our people. Another big piece is that our top brass has some sort of continuity. The last thing the people getting their hands dirty need is for the four star to retire and then the new guy (or girl) comes in and wants things completely different when we are just starting to figure this new system out!

MRU Tip:

Maybe you are new to the unit and there are outstanding people in front of you or you simply understand that in many squadrons it is a total shot in the dark once your name goes to the next level for consideration. Whatever the case, there is one thing that is in your control, and many people do not pay close attention to its importance. So often we see people who figure they are an automatic promote (formally a 3). They think if they just show up for work on time and don't cause any trouble, they will naturally fall into that holding tank I spoke of above. Not only is this terrible thinking, it is also not true. If you default to this line of thinking, you risk your management team giving you a "not ready now." The repercussions to your career for getting this can take a few years to get off your back!

You are in a competition and graded on a curve no matter what you may think. This is a simple truth. As time goes on and we all figure out this evaluation system, more and more people will be receiving this rating and it won't be as much of a career suppressant. But until that day happens, you cannot allow your supervision to sit down and ask whether or not you should be a "not ready now."

It's All About the Words

In a recent poll I questioned 16 chiefs about the promotion boards and suggested that words within the EPR itself where substantially more important than the actual rating. This is clearly due to the holding tank of promotes. This should lead us all to take our time when we are writing our bullets and pay close attention to the level of contribution and impact. Your narrative, as usual in this inflated system, needs to essentially show you as a badass (think Brad Pitt in the movie "Troy"). Never let leadership have the conversation about whether or not you are a not ready now. One of my chief mentors said we should be working on our EPR all year, not just when it's due. Constantly molding our words paints a picture that tells a story. That story should have verbiage with big impact, recognizing the people under you, mentoring those in your community, improving unit processes, and leading people.

Dr. Deming's Deadly Disease

W. Edwards Deming is a leadership and management expert. He is well known and revered. He said annual performance systems are a "deadly disease." Respectively, he believed the same about awards:

they nourish short-term performance, annihilate long-term planning, build fear, demolish teamwork, and nourish rivalry and politics. Does this sound familiar?

In *Total Quality of Performance Appraisal: Choose One*, Peter Scholtes noted, "Improvement efforts should focus on systems, processes, and methods, not on individual workers. Those efforts that focus on improving the attentiveness, carefulness, speed, etc., of individual workers—without changing the systems, processes and methods—constitute a low-yield strategy with negligible short-term results. Conventional problem-solving would ask such questions as: Whose area is this? Who is supposed to replace worn gaskets? We don't ask 'why,' we ask 'who.' We don't look for causes in the system; we look for culprits in the work force. Performance appraisal is a 'who-based' approach to problem solving."

In one short swoop, Scholtes dropped some truth when he boldly stated, "Merit rating rewards people who do well in the system. It does not reward attempts to improve the system. Don't rock the boat."

I challenge everyone to rock the boat. I'm a true believer that all of my Air Force brothers and sisters genuinely want to do well and do the right thing. The system is built to put us all at the starting line of this rat race to promotion. In the end, we need to just kick ass at our jobs, help one another, and challenge the status quo. Slowly, the people who do these things will be the ones being promoted. We can do it together.

Chapter 3

Enlisted Life Management

Goals: Your Destinations in Life

"Begin with the end in mind." — Stephen Covey

Goals are the fuel that allows our journey to begin. But what exactly are they? Wikipedia (damned right I can reference it) defines a goal as a "desired result a person or a system envisions, plans, and commits to achieve; a personal or organizational desired end-point in some sort of assumed development." Put simply, whatever you decide to do for your future is called a goal. This means you are making small goals all the time and may not know it. You see, goals give us focus. Without focus, our potential, abilities, and talent are weak and ineffective. Focusing on something helps us to avoid aimlessly hurling our darts at meaningless tasks.

When you are focused and moving toward something, you can actually measure your success. For example, let's say you are writing a book (see what I did there?). Your *goal* is to write a book and you can measure your progress by how many words you write each day. That becomes a benchmark.

Napoleon Hill, an all-time great life mentor, spoke about the one quality a person must have in order to win. He said that was a definitiveness of purpose fueled with a true, burning desire to achieve. Finding that purpose can feel like choosing what channel to watch, but it is important because it leads to *clarity*. When we find clarity, we are able to avoid deviating from our desires and our goals and objectives become crystal clear.

Get this: Only about 3 percent of us have clear, written goals. If we know that people who have clear, written goals are more successful than everyone else, why not be in that 3 percent? Seems easy, right?

One gigantic barrier in our path is the instinct to grab low-hanging fruit rather than real goals. These are the tasks that are easier, take less time, and give us a sense of artificial satisfaction.

Don't waste your time doing something well that doesn't have a high value.

But you probably already know that having goals is very important, you just haven't gotten around to it or seen the tangible effects it can have on your military career. So I crafted a five-step formula for setting and achieving goals, specifically with the military in mind. Although this is based on my experience in the Air Force, it can be applied to any career. Follow this formula, and you will see your stock rise. But before we check out the formula, something else needs clarification: You must ensure your goals are SMART. Let me break that down for you:

S*pecific:* Generalizing when you're making goals is not cool. Be specific. What exactly do you want to accomplish? What is the time frame? What is the purpose of this goal?

M*easurable*: Clarify your criteria for measuring your progress. It's relevant to stay on track, reach your target dates, and feel those endorphins kick in when you reach a milestone.

A*ction Oriented*: Find ways to make your goals come true is invigorating. You will be surprised at what you can do when you plan your steps wisely and develop the habit of advancing toward the light at the end of the tunnel.

R*ealistic*: You know, I want to be an astronaut too, but is that a realistic goal for me? Not really. With that said, you want to shoot high because the natural motivation that comes with higher goals can propel you further than you may think. Just be willing and able to work, whatever your goal is.

T*imely*: This is where I see a lot of failures. You must have a deadline. If not, where is the sense of urgency? Someday I want to earn a college degree will get you about as far as the astronaut goal. But saying, "By May 15 I will complete the first three credits in

English" will ensure you of some forward motion toward accomplishing your intention.

All right, are you ready for the formula that will drastically improve your life? Follow this and you will find yourself rising to the top of your organization in no time:

1. **Write your goals down.** This seems easy enough, but it just isn't happening. Remember, when you write them down, make them SMART (specific, measurable, attainable, realistic, and timely). When I teach "Preparation for Success" to hundreds of airmen, I always take a goal and ask whether or not it meets this criterion. If it doesn't, then the odds of achieving that goal aren't very good. The final thing to think about when you write down your goals is to decide exactly what you want.

MRU Tip
Ask your supervisor if he will sit down and discuss some clear objectives and tasks and rate them according to the highest significance. This will help get you to get going.

2. **Create milestones**. You need to make deadlines for your goals. Natural procrastination will derail you if you don't set some definite deadlines and milestones. Take your bigger goals and break them down, assigning them subdeadlines if you have to in order to ensure completion. Creating milestones will also organize your goals into priorities.

3. **Make them visible**. I can't tell you how easy it is to write a bunch of goals down only to get snagged after the second one. In the military, we have so many meaningless daily tasks that it's not uncommon to forget about your goals. But if you make them visible, you will be constantly reminded that you have your own deadlines to meet. I place my goals on the whiteboard in my office, on my phone as a reminder that keeps popping up, and on a slip of paper that is always on me. The power of visibility can never be underestimated.

4. **Begin immediately**. Each passing day is another opportunity to move toward success. My chief told me, "You eat an elephant one bite at a time." You would be amazed at how fast you'll accomplish something if you simply start to do it. One thing I know about setting goals is that doing *something*, doing *anything*, is better than doing nothing.

5. **Create a habit**. Doing something every day will help you reach your goals. You want to keep pushing forward and creating some momentum that will transform your life.

My Favorite Habit

When I realized how important habits are, I knew I had to start small in order for something to stick. The typical things we all think of are like waking up earlier, making our bed, going to the gym five times a week, or maybe some sort of quick morning ritual to get the juices flowing. All of these are excellent options, but for me, I wanted a habit that would transform my life while still being what some call a beginner's habit. So I did what Julia Cameron called "spiritual windshield wipers." I decided to journal every morning. I took the advice from Tim Ferriss in Tools of Titans and bought *The Artist's Way: Morning Pages Journal* and haven't looked back since. The windshield wipers quote above is so true, as the words that leave my pen are forever on the paper and their weight is no longer a burden on my day. I don't journal for anyone but me. I recommend everyone should try journaling at least once. If you aren't old school, you can even journal on your phone or other electronic device by using popular applications like *DayOne* (https://dayoneapp.com).

The goals you set and accomplish will set you apart from your peers. It is apparent not many in the enlisted force are thinking big when it comes to goals, because many overestimate what they can accomplish in a year, but they grossly underestimate what they can accomplish in a decade.

> *"Think little goals and expect little achievements.*
> *Think big goals and win big success."*
> —David J. Schwartz

Get Shit Done

I'm not going to sugarcoat it. We all need to get shit done every single day, but most of us have a hard time juggling the million things that are thrown at us. With shifting priorities, the one thing we can always count on in the military, we need simple and effective ways to ensure we are being productive. Isn't it crazy how multitasking—the known enemy of getting shit done—is not only prevalent but encouraged?! How did we let true productivity manifest itself in mediocrity?

Have you ever begun working on something and then your attention was swiftly taken from your target to an email that pops up in front of you? Have you ever been working on random tasks all day and then found yourself with no real sense of accomplishment at the end of the day? Have you ever spent 90 percent of your time on non-value-added items like CBTs (computer-based training) and appointment letters? Me too. Here are a few ways you can get more shit done in your limited time.

Do/Doing/Done

Simple, sure. But in the quicksand of Air Force life, simple is the key to airpower. Okay, maybe not airpower, but it is definitely the key to getting shit done. The Do/Doing/Done board is nothing new. But I adopted it and brought it into my organization because of its potential impact on empowering people while simultaneously maintaining short-to medium-term tasks so projects come to life. Superior to a simple checklist, the Do/Doing/Done board uses Post-it notes to show what we need to do, what we are currently doing, and what is done. In three columns, one column for each, write down the task or project on a sticky note and place it on the board. There are several reasons this is an effective tool:

1. You generate so many ideas each day, and you need a place to put them (in the Do column), which helps you to not lose track. You can call this the "backburner" if you want to get Chuck Norris with it.

2. Celebrating wins is a critical component to a team's success. When we see another sticky made it to the Done column, it makes us want to do a Tiger Woods fist pump.

3. Empowering your people means giving them tangible opportunities. The way we do this is by allowing all the people in the organization to manage the board. At any point, the lowest airman can write something on a sticky and place it on the board. Another key point is that people can attach themselves to any task or project they like, based on their own interests. That a huge deal!

4. Adding a few elements to the Doing column can make a huge difference. Consider categories based on strategic impact. Put another way, how much energy are you applying to each of the Post-its in the Doing column? I use three categories, currently *Extreme*, *Medium*, and Idle, with Extreme being the tasks with that the highest impact and needing high energy now.

Bringing the Do/Doing/Done board to life requires very little effort, and the rewards can be astonishing. The final piece of this "get shit done" trick is to attach an Outlook task to the bigger projects, with specifics. There is nothing more annoying than having a project with no action steps. Attaching a person or people to the project via Outlook keeps you organized and alleviates the need to micromanage status updates. What are you waiting for? Go make yourself a Do/Doing/Done board!

Three to Thrive

Every morning on my short drive to work, I turn down the volume on my Joe Rogan podcast and work through my "Three to Thrive." These are three things that—no matter what the day decides to throw at me—will get done. I learned about this from motivational speaker Tony Robbins during a YouTube session that likely started with something like "Fail videos 2016."

I write those three things on stickies and place them in front of me on the board so I can see them throughout the day. Determining to get those three things done does so much for my confidence and helps me prioritize the things that matter from the things that don't.

MRU Tip

Have your people write down on a sticky note one thing they will do before they go home that day. Let them come up with it and they will own it. Place it on the board. Everyone holds everyone accountable for knocking out their one thing. It really works.

How to Make Your Supervisor Love You

> *Any supervisor worth his salt would rather deal with people who attempt too much than with those who try too little.* —Lee Iacocca

The Real Golden Rule

When we were in grade school, we learned about the Golden Rule: Do unto others as you would want them to do to you." This applies not just in kindergarten but throughout your entire life. But in the military, there is a different set of rules. In fact, it's a whole different world when you are active duty, so knowing what the rules are is critical to being successful. Over the years I have gained a better understanding of what this new rule set is all about and how to prioritize which are more important than others. I've concluded there is, indeed, a new Golden Rule while serving, and that rule is "Always remember who feeds you."

Who feeds you? Your rich Uncle Sam? Your commander? Your Peers? No. Your supervisor is the one who has the most influence over your career. He or she is the first in line to make or break you. Your direct supervisor does the one thing that carries the most weight on promotion potential: your EPR.

This Golden Rule must be observed at all times. When two people need something, and one is your supervisor, the priority always goes to your supervisor. Doesn't matter if the other person outranks them. Sure, you will do both tasks, but the rater gets preferential treatment. Moreover, when you have a billion emails flooding your in-box (and we all know we don't have enough space on that thing), how do you check them? Which are more important? Your supervisor's are! I make it a point to filter my supervisor's name along with my flight chief's in order to be swift with my response. This has proven to be very valuable.

No, this isn't kissing ass. This is providing the most influential person in your military life the respect he or she deserves and showing that you are prompt and efficient, along with demonstrating a clear pattern of reliability. Leadership is influenced by what you do, but having an advocate who directly rates you is huge and will go a long way.

In the end, it is your supervisor who promotes you in staff meetings. It is he or she who can give their time to mentoring or developing you or simply letting you figure it out on your own. They will be the ones in the trenches, fighting for your place at the top of the forced distribution list. So do yourself a big favor and live the new Golden Rule of the military: Always remember who feeds you.

Love Birds: The Supervisor and the Subordinate

Your job as a subordinate is fairly straightforward: lighten your leader's load. I often find it rather comical how easy it is to get ahead in the Air Force. You just need to do the diligence of seeing things through and volunteer to take on the organizational challenges. How often do you see ratees ask for feedback? How often do you see ratees write down expectations for their supervisor? Not too often. This is sad, because if you do this, your supervisor will respond. For you young ones, guess what? We aren't any different than you. In fact, most supervisors aren't remotely as competent or intelligent as their subordinates. Surprise! If you assert yourself as someone with ambitions, and you are truly motivated to do what it takes to succeed and move your unit forward, you will swiftly rise to the top. It is inevitable.

But whatever you do, don't kiss ass! Your supervisor will see right through that. I like the people who couldn't care less what their supervisor thinks and just kicks ass all the time, helping others consistently and always signing up for the tough jobs. Those things get noticed quickly and act as some sort of reverse psychology on supervisors.

MRU Tip

If you think you should be considered for an award, fill out the 1206 yourself and send it to your supervisor. The email should read something along these lines: "Sir/Ma'am, I feel this has been an exceptional quarter. If you believe I have earned it, I would like the attached package to be considered."

If you do this, I don't know a supervisor in the world who wouldn't want to move you up for consideration. The fact you did their work for them is even more ammo. We must remember that human beings love to have things done for them. If you do the work, there's a higher probability it will go somewhere. Relying on your supervisor to unfailingly take care of you and do the labor of putting together something to help your career is never a wise decision.

What's the Feedback on Feedback?

Sometimes you may be the supervisor. There is nothing more important than showing your peeps that you care than to conduct a methodical, two-way feedback session. Here are four great tips for using your feedback to create momentum:

1. Assign specific goals. Employees who receive specific goals usually perform better than those who do not.

2. Assign measurable goals. Put goals in quantitative terms and include target dates or deadlines. If measurable results will not be available, then satisfactory completion (such as "satisfactorily attended workshop") is the next best thing.

3. Assign challenging but doable goals. Goals should be challenging, but not so difficult they appear unrealistic.

4. Encourage participation. Managers often wonder if they should tell their employees what their goals are or let them participate in setting their goals. Evidence suggests that participating in setting goals does not consistently result in higher performance than assigned goals, but assigned goals do not consistently result in

higher performance than participative ones. It is only when the participants set goals higher than the assigned ones that the participants produce higher performance. Because it tends to be easier to set higher standards when your employees participate, contribution tends to lead to improved performance.

How to Win BTZ

"BTZ is not important except in the impact it has on other lives."
— A. J. Kehl

Within the first few months of your being at a new station, before you even know that the upstairs bathroom is much cleaner than the one downstairs, everyone will be talking about how to win below the zone (BTZ). According to the most credible source ever, namely, Wikipedia, BTZ is a competitive early promotion program offered to enlisted personnel in the grade of Airman First Class/E-3. This early promotion opportunity is restricted to elite airmen who stand out from their peers and perform duties at a level above their current rank.

In other words, if you are doing well in your performance, this program gives you an opportunity to quick promote. Or as we used to think of it, "not eat Top Ramen anymore." This incentive provides an opportunity to be a leader among your peers, but these dudes really just want to make a little more money and have an extra stripe.

Before jumping into how you can place yourself in an advantageous position to win this award, I confess I did not win BTZ. In fact, I don't even remember being eligible, because it is contingent on your supervisor writing a package for consideration, and apparently I sucked.

I have many years of experience with this topic and can offer some advice on this opportunity, which I'm biased about in a negative way.

Three Ways to Win BTZ

1. Finish your career development courses (CDCs) faster than the next guy. In one of the most ridiculous forms of measurement, many NCOs ramble on about how their guy is done with Set 3 of their CDCs and yours is still on Set 2. Never mind they should

not be rushed to learn their job and fully understand it. Instead, this race of all hares is a catalyst for the BTZ conversation.

2. Have an NCO known for his fine writing. Like many awards in the Air Force, it's all about how the package is written, not necessarily the quality of the person's performance behind the package.

3. Dominate the board. Face-to-Face boards are unfavorable to those without a presence. Being confident, calm, and deliberate in your answers will be the difference between earning a third stripe and not. I have sat on these boards before, and confidence is key. Know about the Air Force. Know about AFI 1-1 and AFI 36-2618. Good luck!

If you win BTZ, don't be surprised if your peers are salty. Everyone loves average. If you show progress quicker than your friends, especially at such a young point in your career, there is typically a minor uptick in jealousy from those you want support from. You are expected to lead the very people you were learning *with*.

In the end, I wouldn't put too much emphasis on winning BTZ. Instead, focus on really learning your role and your job's functions. Be the best at what you do and things will come in due time. If you get caught up too early in the rat race, it can cause too much unneeded stress. If it makes you feel any better, I did a poll in the summer of 2016 by asking 50 master sergeants who made E-7 in under 14 years if they had won BTZ. Of the 50, only 7 said they had. That's only 14 percent. My assumption is the other 86 percent were consistent in being really great at their job, and the tortoise won yet again.

Promote Me!

"People don't get promoted for doing their jobs really well. They get promoted by demonstrating their potential to do more."
— Tara Jayne Frank

In a world where legitimate power holds the majority share within the organization, promotion is the key to having greater influence across your unit and wing. Everyone wants to promote, of course, but the majority simply don't understand what it takes to move up the enlisted ranks. Now, that doesn't mean I know it all or anything, it just means there is a certain path that increases your probability. Through the years I have seen many people promote only to find out it is extremely difficult to pinpoint what exactly makes a person promotable. Is it the one who is out there, across the wing? The one who everyone knows and can see is involved in everything? Or is it the one who stays in their lane, focusing on being a true technical expert? The answer comes as no surprise that it is a little of each of these—and more.

Promotion to staff sergeant is simply a matter of attrition. I know it is a huge deal, but the fact is that everyone will make staff sergeant, that is, if they don't totally jack up their career. Making staff sergeant early is awesome, except for the fact that those who make it quickly (within three to four years) typically aren't ready to be an NCO. Under the new system (which is covered later in this chapter), at least members are prioritized, so hopefully the best ones are promoted. Even though I paint the staff sergeant picture as one where it's just about being present, that doesn't mean the things you are (or aren't) doing aren't important. If you understand the way things work at an early stage in your career, you will go much farther—or at least much faster!

The technical sergeant step is a steep hill where you need to actually be worthwhile. This is the stage where you will be putting yourself in a position to leap forward to the next level quickly if you do things correctly. They say making technical sergeant is the hardest rank you make in the enlisted force, and I'm not calling whoever "they" are liars, either. When I made technical sergeant, the rate of promotion was around 18 percent in my career field.

If you didn't already know before reading this book, master sergeant includes an addition to the whole testing game. That's right, boards. And dominating the board is the difference maker. It is a true pendulum where you can get destroyed on one side or leapfrog the other supervisors around you. I will do my best to go over the boards in detail for you below, hopefully providing you with the information and secrets you need to being successful when your time comes.

As you move through this chapter, remember that I'm merely a Senior Master Sergeant, so I really can't tell you how the hell you make chief. Lucky for us though, I brought in some chiefs to fill in that gap!

Job Performance

Your mission should come first, obviously. There is one way to be successful in knowing your job, and that is to fully understand the regulations and guides that govern what you do. Nothing is more annoying than someone who doesn't know the technical aspects of their *one* job. Ever go into Military Personnel Flight (MPF) and ask a question, only for a senior airman to turn around and ask the NCO? I always think, "Dude, this is a basic question about *your* job." This leads me to a rooted issue in the military: ownership. How many people take pride in their job and do whatever it takes to be the best at it? Maybe I'm wrong and should continue to be an optimist here, but I often get the feeling that people are not very diligent in understanding their roles.

You (yes, you!) can make a difference right off by focusing on tying your job to getting planes in the air, troops on the front lines, or whatever the case may be. This could be considered the first step toward taking ownership. If we had more ownership and pride across the board, there would be less bitching about how Joe Shmoe is always volunteering. When someone is a badass at their job, no one will say anything about their volunteering or taking of College Level Examination Program exams (CLEPs).

Your job is numero uno, and before you do anything else, know your job. Once you are performing at a high level, then do other things and mute those haters who will still try to bring you down for being well rounded.

Significant Self-Improvement

The Air Force is rapidly becoming a true business corporation. Headlining issues like "Blues Mondays" is just the start of an institutional move in that direction (whatever that direction is). The Air Force you knew eight years ago has been strategically pushed aside to make way for this leaner, with a dash of salt, smarter service. It is in this service that certain things matter more than they did not so long ago, and one of those steps to success in today's Air Force is still *free*.

Education is more important than ever. Is it more important than your job? Dumb question. Of course not. It is, however, a way that delineates winners from average joes. Did I mention it is free?! Like my dad always said, "If you aren't growing, you're dying." Just as in business, you must continue to grow your knowledge base, and being educated is fundamental to this.

Education Is Key

I'm no smarter than anyone else. In fact, I often wonder why my brain doesn't do some of the things other people's brains can do. But you don't need to be a genius to see that education in the Air Force has gone from:

2003: "I am a master sergeant and working on my CCAF so I can make senior."

2018: "I am a master sergeant working on my bachelor's so I can make senior."

Fact is, education matters. Don't believe me? How can you distinguish yourself from everyone else when everything on paper looks the same? When someone is judging you for a promotion or award, how can they tell you apart from someone else? The answer has many parts: breadth of experience, awards, community involvement, and—you guessed it—education. You may not agree with me on this, but if education isn't an important factor, how come it is always on your EPR, your Career Data Brief, and your SURF (single unit retrieval format)? We must understand there is a bottleneck here. You cannot move up without moving.

In a world where many more people are getting their CCAF earlier, you must take the next step: bachelor's.

Like I said earlier, I'm not that smart. But I have mastered the art of pressure, and it has gotten me to a place where I have a master's and I haven't spent a single measly dollar. If you throw a nickel in a jar once a month, eventually it adds up to a dollar, right? Same goes with education. You don't need to be over-aggressive with it. Just be consistent.

Pressure

You must pressure yourself by getting in there, setting up a degree plan, closing your eyes, and pressing Submit TA Request. Once that happens, you can no longer procrastinate, because money is on the line! (If you fail a class, you owe the money back.) Forget the excuses. Stop saying you don't have the time. Don't even think. Just click Submit.

Still, according to a recent Government Accountability Office study, only 36 percent of active duty Air Force members are using this benefit. Makes you wonder what the other 64 percent were crying about when TA (tuition assistance) was briefly taken away, doesn't it?

Uncle Sam spends $540 million a year on this amazing program. Get your piece of the pie! Your career and promotion may depend on it.

Community Relations

Private Organizations Pay Mad Dividends

Damn right! Hopefully you didn't forget that your network is your net worth. As you began your journey through this chicken scratch, you found out that who you know rather than who knows you is critical to being successful in both life and the enlisted military. Private organizations fill that void and provide unique opportunities to grow.

First of all, if you are an NCO, it lays this out for you in AFI 36-2618 (the little brown book). Basically, you have no choice as the good ole Air Force says that this is a minimum requirement. I can't tell you how many times I have sat in a 5/6 meeting and there were only 15 people in there when the wing has a truckload of NCOs. To clarify a bit, 5/6 is usually the name of the NCO tier private organization. They focus on professional growth and mentorship and provide the whole community with all sorts of events and opportunities. This organization is wing level, which means you should be a part of it! Being a part of smaller organizations is awesome, and I think it's a great idea for you to join. But if you know, as an NCO, simply being a part of them is a minimum, why wouldn't you maximize by trying to be an executive officer?

Here is a tip that worked pretty well for me. If you are reading this and you are an NCO, run for an executive spot on the 5/6 council. Vice president is the best spot, because the poor president has to do a thousand times what you have to do and you get to learn from them (good and bad). Too many people are afraid of being on the executive council and I don't know why. The water may look cold, but screw it. Jump in!

But what if you're not an NCO?

This is the time to learn! Airman councils are begging for leadership among their peers. If you are looking for a way to separate yourself, learn about private organizations early so you can make mistakes that have little impact. I bet you could make a call right now and get on the council. That's how badly they need it.

Private organizations are not the be-all end-all deal that will get you promoted. But the thing is, when the Chief Master Sergeant of the Air Force wants us to write in the "Whole Airman Concept" line on the EPR, this has a lot of what they are talking about. Specifically, for those who are being boarded, it is crucial to hold an executive officer position on all three weighted EPRs. If you can't do all three, the top two hold most of the weight, so be sure it is on there. When you are being boarded, they want leadership. When you are an executive officer, you are leading people from all different jobs. Winner, winner, chicken dinner!

The following are my picks:

1. Any of the tiered councils: This includes ACE/First Four, 5/6 and Top III. These are the heavy hitters and are a must for your record.

2. Air Force Sergeants Association: Of all the organizations, this is the one I most believe in. Check out the private organizations appendix at the back of the book for more information.

3. Air Force Association: This organization can never get off the ground at the local level, but it has big-time impact across the Air Force. Taking the lead on this council can reap some big, personally rewarding benefits.

Promotion and the Power of Habit

A long time ago, Aristotle brilliantly said, *"You are what you repeatedly do."* He got that right. Our habits, both good and bad, define us. Habits can bring you down or raise you up. The key to success is forming habits that are in line with your goals, both short and long term.

When I think of a habit that can help you in the military, I think of people who wake up early to get in some physical training (PT). My friend Brandon Johnson, through the power of habit, easily wakes up before the sun peaks over the horizon and dominates the gym. Sometimes he runs, sometimes he lifts weights. He has formed a habit that basically guarantees success when it comes time for his PT test.

Another habit is procrastination and its detrimental effect on our potential.

Aside from PT, there's another habit that will generally guarantee you promotion. This habit is so simple, so obvious, and yet the majority of people dismiss it or only give it a fraction of the attention it deserves. This habit is called study. Yeah, I know. Crazy, right!?

All jokes aside, *you* can promote up to technical sergeant (E-6) by simply being one of the minority that actually studies. Now, when I say study, I don't mean cracking the PDG (Professional Development Guide) a month prior to your test date and expecting positive results. This isn't a get-rich-quick type of deal. It's a slow, methodical recipe. The fact is that people don't give it 100 percent.

I asked many people who are eligible for promotion how their studying is going. Many nonchalantly shrug a shoulder and say, "Eh, it's going." Crazy! This is a step toward many important things, and an increase in pay is the least of these.

I didn't truly allow this habit to flourish until I was a staff sergeant studying for technical sergeant. I, like others, simply believed that if I studied close to the exam date, I would be able to cram enough info into my noggin to pass. This is a terrible idea!

Here Is the Secret

The one habit you must form is this: Delete all distractions from your life. Yes, all of them. I learned this from a fast burner in my career field that made all the ranks through senior master sergeant the first time. I asked him at a flight Christmas party, "What's the secret?"

He said, "You have to look around and do what others aren't. I told my wife I would not be available for things like partying, get-togethers, TV, nothing. If it didn't have to do with PDG [the professional development guide] or SKT [specialty knowledge test], then I didn't want to hear about it."

At first, I thought, Yeah, right. We have lives and families and we can't do that. But that's not true. We can and we must. Dismissing everything that's irrelevant will have you adding a stripe in a few short months. That's a return on investment.

Since forming this habit, I have made the last three ranks back-to-back, and all I did was ensure I was focused. When others played video games, I studied. When others slept, I studied. Just study.

The exact formula I used going through the sections in the professional development guide (PDG) involved the Military Knowledge and Testing System (MKTS) (a survey of what others think is important test material). I would go through a section and then take the quiz on that section in the PDG advisor software program. If I answered a question incorrectly, I would highlight it in a different color than the highlight color I used during my first reading. After I went through each section, I changed my morning routine to wake up 60 minutes earlier and do a chapter in PDG Gold. By the time I completed all the tests for PDG Gold, I had read every chapter three times. Aside from that particular study habit, I wanted to be selective in *how* I studied. What do I mean? Well, why even study heritage and history? I read it because it interested me and it is a part of our traditions, but for promotion it is a waste of time. Instead, I spent extra time on the more important chapters, because at the end of the day, you don't want to invest hours of your time for a single question or two (who knows how many you will see).

Another strategy is to limit your time. Your brain, well, my brain, cannot retain anything after a while. I *always* study in 20-minute intervals. Never play any of the games! (They are a waste of your time.)

In the end, you either want it or you don't. The majority will not do what it takes to know the material, and that opens the door of opportunity for you. Like my Dad (and greatest mentor) said, "You are just as entitled to it as anyone else." That goes with many things in life, and promotion (at least the testing part) is no exception. Remember, Aristotle hooked us up. So create and maintain habits that allow you to go into the testing center with a confident smile on your face.

Six Splendid Ways to Study for Promotion

So what is that elusive recipe for success? Well, everyone is different. Some play games. Some just read the Airman's Manual. (By the way, why not just print it out like before? I will most likely still use the printer at work.) Don't act like you don't!

I have asked around and found it is truly different for everyone, but there are a few ways to make sure you are on the correct path, and, as usual, My Rich Uncle has your back. From setting the mood to finding out how *you* learn, here are six splendid ways to study for that stripe:

1. www.brain.fm: Get lifetime access for cheap. This also will get you in the zone https://www.reddit.com/r/ADHD/comments/3s0sq1/have_any_of_you_used_brainfm_its_really_helping

2. http://vark-learn.com/the-vark-questionnaire/: How do you learn? Find out here.

3. Don't just study the End of Course Exam (EOC) questions in your specialty knowledge tests (SKTs), read the chapter and then answer the questions. This goes with PDG too! Don't be lazy. Read!

4. Block out one to two hours a night to study, two to four on weekends, and take ten-minute breaks at least once an hour. If nights don't work for you, do the morning thing. Just remember, you won't retain much after a while.

5. Take off a week or two before the test (leave) and don't study a damned thing a day or two before the test. Is a little bit of leave worth that pay increase? Hell, yeah it is!

6. Show up early, and when you are done, go back to your car and write down every question you can remember and look them up later. Give yourself one point for each one you got right (obviously) and a half point for each one you think you got right. Whenever I did this, I was able to remember at least 80 percent of the questions and came within 10 points of my actual score. Plus, I had a pretty damned good study guide for next year—just in case.

There are many ways to study, and this is just the tip of the iceberg (dead ahead). But, hey, hopefully you take a thing or two from this and get a better score this year. Big thanks to Pa Tom for the hookup.

Feeding Your Brain for Testing

Have you heard of nootropics? They are loopholes when it comes to enhancing your cognitive abilities. These bad boys are just another way to gain an edge when it comes to WAPS (weighted airman promotion system) testing or brain power in general. A quick flip through Webster's and you'll see it's defined as drugs, supplements, or other substances that improve cognitive function, particularly executive functions, memory, creativity, or motivation, in healthy individuals. Umm, yes, please.

I heard about them on one of my favorite podcasts, The Joe Rogan Experience, and I immediately wanted to see what they were and if they actually worked. Joe (I call him Joe because we are cool like that) says to take this preloaded pill by Onnit Labs called Alpha Brain. This is a great way to begin using nootropics, and there were definitely differences with my sharpness. When I take it first thing in the morning, I'm razor sharp until around 10:00 a.m. Is this some lame gimmick? Maybe. Maybe not. Alpha Brain has been through various clinical trials and is proven to increase:

Verbal memory
Processing speed
Peak alpha (flow state)

After seeing some pretty nice results while using it, I knew the time had come to take it a step further and see what kind of stack I would want to use for a big test. This was in October 2014, and my WAPS test for master sergeant was just a few months out. In order to get my scores up, I needed effective study habits, a well-balanced diet (which I suck at), and something else, namely, nootropics! They made me feel so awesome that I found myself making loud noises when my fingers struck the keys on a keyboard. This was going to be one hell of a testing year.

Ensuring I was not breaking any laws became the first step in experimenting with nootropics.

Nootropics achieve their effects by altering the supply of neurochemicals, enzymes, and hormones in the brain. At first glance, this seems a little crazy, but it's really the word that has the broad, often confusing definition. You see, as there has been a rise in the use of these legal brain boosters, there has also been a widening definition under this general umbrella. Nootropics can be anything from boring old ginseng to stuff I wouldn't even attempt to pronounce. Before the latest surge in popularity, nootropics were basically like caffeine and jacking up your intake of fish oil, both of which have some sound science to back them up.

To be honest, it's wise to stay away from anything controversial. First, there are always some dudes trying to ruin your day or, in this case, your brain high. Second, why get in trouble and possibly ruin your career? It isn't worth it. I stayed away from the crazy stacks and decided to use Alpha Brain, GO Cubes by Nootrobox, and fish oil. I didn't feel like Bradley Cooper in Limitless or anything, but I felt an uptick in my ability to reach back and pull out some information. Basically, I was a boss.

Before I go into how the test went and all, I want to say I'm not endorsing the use of nootropics. If you want to join the growing community of "Nooaunts," that's your deal. I also should point out you may very well improve your scores by, you know, studying. When I tell my friends about nootropics, I hear they may try it, but they have seen similar results by eating a grip of blueberries and dark chocolate. Do whatever floats your boat.

Walking into the test, I was ready to kill it. The questions on the PFE (primary developmental education) exam were crystal clear, like I was digesting some Taco Bell after a day without food. I would stuff my brain with the information, and the answers were ready before I even looked at the options. For the first time in my career, I zoomed through a test, ultimately scoring an 89 percent. For my SKT (specialty knowledge test), it wasn't as great, but my 72 percent was 10 points higher than it had ever been before. Boom!

Now, either I'm the most superstitious guy ever (more so than Robert De Niro in "Silver Linings Playbook" where if he moved the remote control to the left, the Eagles would lose) or I'm actually onto something. Whether you believe nootropics work or not is irrelevant, because you can easily read about them and see that science backs this stuff up. Whether or not you use it to your advantage when taking your WAPS (weighted airman promotion system) test is totally up to you. My job is to simply look at ways you can maximize your enlistment.

PME Doesn't Suck

Two years into this journey, I heard about professional military education (PME), and the negativity that surrounded it was robust. There's always a few people saying things like, "Oh, yeah, I have to go to ALS [Airman Leadership School]. This is gonna be so lame." Even the NCOs were talking shit. By year three I was thinking how terrible it must be and how it would be a toned-down repeat of basic training. I could see it now: a bunch of people yelling at you for no reason while you find time in between the drilling and PT to learn about stupid military stuff. This was going to really suck!

Per the youj (my attempt at making the word usual sound cool), these people were wrong. It seems most of the negativity that surrounds PME and any form of military education is dead wrong. In fact, PME is one of the best times I have had in any educational environment, and it is only getting better with time.

You can maximize your enlistment through PME.

The number-one thing PME offers is opportunities to speak in front of people. You may have not seen that coming, but don't forget that speaking in front of crowds is the number-one thing most people are afraid of. Well, in both ALS and Non-Commissioned Officer Academy (NCOA), you don't have a choice, and this pressure is perfect for you to overcome this fear. Speaking is so critical to growth, and I leverage it at every opportunity. Want more? Join Toastmasters International, the club where a bunch of people meet and develop their speaking skills. Pretty sweet in my opinion.

The second-most important thing PME offers you is the ability to meet new, interesting people. ALS was just the starting point. Seven years have gone by and I still keep in touch with a few of them. Seeing them grow is pretty cool, and our times in ALS really created some deep bonds. If nothing else, PME cultivates relationships.

The third thing PME offers from a maximization point is that you can graduate with different awards, including the Levitow Award, the Commandant's Award, and the Distinguished Graduate Award. Do these matter? I don't know. I admit I never earned any of these, but I know those who did had a pretty gnarly bullet on that next EPR, the kind that gets you promoted.

Before we go any further, you need to understand those awards aren't guarantees in any way. It sure didn't hurt me or any others that have been promoted quickly. It is something, though, that can wedge an edge for you when it comes time to rack and stack you against the others in your unit.

My memory is sharp when I think back on how many times someone on the board said, "Hey, this guy got the Levitow," followed by rambling approval. It is one of those shiny pennies that puts the icing on the promotion cake. So how can you earn one? Well, for one, you need to be crushing those awkward, ambiguous tests. You also need to always look super sharp in uniform and have a reputation as a known leader in your flight. There will be many graded sections during the lessons, and you will be required to perform well on those as well. Oh, yeah, they include a lot of speaking, so clear your throat.

Like all things military, the meat is in the details. Pay close attention to the small ways you can distinguish yourself as someone who is there to grow and help.

Here are a few tips to get you started:

- On the first day of class, create a group chat on Facebook or WhatsApp and get everyone on there.

- Next, put together a notebook on Evernote or OneNote and share it with everyone in the class. This really helped everyone out, and I just randomly thought of it at NCOA. When you make a notebook, everyone can share their notes and such. It is such a cool way to collaborate!

- Finally, be the person who steps up and hosts after-class teaching sessions for those who want to refine what they've learned. By teaching others, you will also ensure that the information is tightly stored in that hard drive in your brain.

Another, even greater benefit of doing this is the fact you are really helping people! They will be appreciative of your time. My flight in NCOA didn't win any major awards, but we were the only flight where everyone passed the final test. Go Eagle flight! #Missyourfaces.

Breakdown

ALS: Airman Leadership School is for those who are about to take that leap to become an NCO. It is a brief moment of time where you are "re-blued" and then thrown to the wolves.

NCOA: Non-Commissioned Officer Academy, or as I call it, freaking awesome time academy, is going to be pretty much all technical sergeants. What a good time it is! Take advantage of this time, network with the people around you, and become a black rope, because you get out of most cleaning and admin stuff.

SNCO: Senior Non-Commissioned Officer Academy is where the big boys are out to get their PME on. Those who are senior master sergeants or have a line number attend this academy. Some may not know this, but you can attend without a line number as well, depending on your overall score and availability.

Professional Military Education is a staple for your success in the military. It is one of those nuances that can really take a chunk out of your future if you don't take it seriously. If you don't believe that, you should speak with some of the people I know who recently procrastinated on Course 15 (before you read any further, search "hitler course 15" on YouTube).

Courses 14 and 15 are the precursors to in-residence PME that we love to hate. There is a mountain of information with severe implications if you don't take the time to knock it out. I recently went to a local education center and found that, on average, people are waiting until the last minute to schedule their first test for Course 15 (or the new DLC [distance learning course]). You should be dominating this thing right out of the gate or it will wear you down. While you are studying, don't forget your scores will carry over like those Verizon minutes when it's time to go to an actual classroom.

When all the PME cards are turned over, you will find that PME doesn't suck. It is a premiere opportunity to establish lifelong friends and some of the material is very relevant. In particular, the sections on negotiations and full-range leadership development should earn your attention as they become yet another 10MB of data in your hard drive the brain.

Why Awards Do Matter

*"I don't deserve this award, but I have arthritis and
I don't deserve that either."* — Jack Benny

The Secret of Quarterly Awards

I know, I know. Don't be wood sharks. It seems no one likes the one who is clearly trying to win awards. The whole transactional thing (we will talk about that later) is pretty lame. Some people simply thrive off awards. Awards are a funny thing. If you avoid them, you watch people pass you by who may be a lower caliber than you. At the same time, if you understand their importance and you remain competitive by submitting a package, you are a "wood chucker." What the hell is that all about?! It is a true catch-22, a double-edged sword. The trick is to get someone else to submit one on your behalf. But how do you do that once you are, say, a senior non-commissioned officer (SNCO)?

The system is set up so awards actually matter. Think about this: When the board is looking over your package for promotion consideration, they only have a minute or so to look at all of you. How the hell is that even possible? I spoke with a few chiefs who were on the board last year, and they said that all they have time for is to scan the impact and read the last *two* bullets (those should be your hardcore bullets) on your EPR. Now, if that is all they are looking at, which do you think will have the greatest influence on your score?

Impact 1: "lauded by Command Chief"

Impact 2: "MSG NCO of the 2nd Qtr"

It is pretty evident which is greater. Now, I understand not everyone can get awards, nevertheless the point remains: awards matter. Feel free to say how stupid they are (which they are) and go to the roof of your uniformly brown building and scream so even The Fired Up Chief can hear you. In the end, awards will continue to play a significant role in career advancement.

Should they play such a large role? Well, the point of recognition is to point out who the go-to players are. In a perfect world, this makes sense and they should most definitely have an edge come promotion time. The problem, however, is this isn't the way it works. How often do we see someone who is not the best of the best take home the hardware? Probably more often than not.

With the understanding we must have integrity in the system, we need to better position ourselves to receive an award (if deserving). This starts with your supervisor. This is the person who—if you are truly performing—should be doing their part to submit you. Let me hit you with a quick story.

I knew a guy who was truly bleeding blue. I mean this guy probably had giant Hap Arnold wings tattooed across his chest! He was doing everything right. Dominated at his job, a noble community leader, and dropping college credits like it was the cool thing to do. The only problem is that he was a technical sergeant, and there was no one to do the right thing and nominate him for awards. He believed if his supervision didn't submit him, then he must not be deserving. Although virtuous, this ended up costing him quite a bit. His peers, his subordinates, leapfrogged him because they simply submitted awards. This guy was truly deserving, and he was totally shafted. This *never* happens in our Air Force!

We clearly know awards are important whether you like it or not.

Here Is How to Create an Edge in the Awards System

Awards are given quarterly. There are four quarters in a year, and within your flight there are typically a few different categories based off the tier in which you fall. For the sake of illustration, let's just go with airman, NCO, and SNCO. One person from each category goes up to the squadron for award consideration. Which quarter do you think is the best to go after? Do you think it matters? I do.

The first quarter is the *only* quarter you should be going after.

At the end of each year you have the annual awards. The person who won fourth quarter admittedly has a slight advantage because it is fresh, but that isn't really a big deal. Only in time in grade (TIG) years should you care too much about annuals anyway. The first quarter is the one you want to target, because everyone has pretty much forgotten about awards after the annuals have been awarded. Annual awards are almost always late, meaning they are done in February or March for the previous year. This adds to the perception that this is the only award that should be sought after, even though it is in the middle of the first quarter. I found the competition is *much* less in this quarter than any other, and that has paid off. I have won the first quarter in all but one of my quarterly awards throughout my career. Boom!

Awards no one thinks about is another way to seriously increase your stock. People focus on the wing annual awards, but there is chaos there because of stiff competition. When you are trying to perform effectively at your mission, you don't want to have to deal with all of that. For me, I wanted to be the best firefighter in the world. I can only dream of a day when the awards system doesn't skew the data. That just isn't the case, and I understand that. I hope you do too, if you want to truly maximize your enlistment.

You might think, How many should I win in order to have the edge? The answer is that it depends. With the new EPR changes that took effect in 2016, board members are only looking five years back as opposed to the previous dive 10 years back. This means the Air Force wants to know, "What have you done for me lately?" This is a good thing if you are just now reading this awesome book and wanting to get your head out of your ass, but it can also hurt you if you emptied the tank too early. Remember the top EPR is worth 60 percent, so you want to make sure you have, at a minimum, a quarterly award at the squadron level during your time-in-grade eligible year. I want to foot stomp (I never liked that expression) the whole minimum thing. Once you are a SNCO, you need to get past the squadron level or you may be kissing that top 3.5 percent away.

On the other hand, Big Blue only looking back five years helps a lot of people who have less than perfect markings, say, seven years ago. I knew a guy who had an Article 15 from years back, and it just killed him under the old system. But with the five-year dive, they couldn't see that blemish, and he ended up making master sergeant right away. Good for him!

The Key to a 1206

Spending very little time, I can tell you the key to using that 1206 to snatch another trophy is doing things above your level. How dumb. Dumb, that is, but true. The competition is doing things above their level, so how can you have a fighting chance if you aren't doing the same? Luck of the Irish? Not this time.

The emphasis on job performance and leadership cannot be understated, but it also has to have some delectable icing on the top. You know what I mean, those bottom categories. Although I don't agree with it, there were so many times I sat on an awards board and heard people say things like, "Well, I figure if they won at the SQ, they must be good at their job" and "If they got this far, I don't even look at the job stuff, just at the community involvement and self-improvement." You can throw the bullshit flag if you want, but I say this very truly.

SAD FACT: If you aren't an executive for a private organization *and* going to college, you will have a hard time winning once it goes to the big leagues (Group/Wing).

If you do something, what are you doing to improve it? What metrics can you use to illustrate you have dominated what was done before? What are you doing every day to improve your process to a point where it is an Air Force Specialty Code (AFSC) or Air Force benchmark?

MRU TIP

Never stop at your flight. If you've made something really special, get it to the next level up. When I created the Workspace platform for the Fire Department to conduct its business affairs, I wasn't satisfied with the flight having an easier life; I wanted the Air Force to have an easier way of doing business. This isn't because I'm any smarter than anyone else; it's because of the mind-set and that alone. This kind of stuff is what stands out on a 1206.

My peer did six credits this quarter? I'll do nine. You get the point.

The 1206 is something you should be taking your time on. The most important part of your individual process of writing a package is to have several people you trust look it over. Yes, they will bleed on it with red pens and make you question why you let them see it in the first place, but it will usually be for good reason, because the 1206—writing bullets in general—is not English but art. It is art that only comes with experience. You know that guy who is the best damned bullet writer but sees nothing but squiggly red lines under every word in an essay? Get him. He knows the art. He is a Picasso of bullets and will help you get out of the minor leagues.

Don't Be a Scam!

The biggest scam in the Air Force is and will always be the awards system. We all know this, so don't add to the pile of people out there who do whatever they have to do to make themselves look good. There are people out there who will straight up steal bullets, purposely arrive at the right time when the distinguished visitor happens to enter the building, and basically stomp skulls to get ahead. These people are a systemic cancer that must be stopped and called out. Don't be those guys! Instead, be the person who works harder than everyone else. If they arrive at 0730, you need to arrive at 0700. If they perform at a decent level, you need to perform at a superior level. The point is, awards will come if you remain diligent in all you do. With that said, you will know you are doing well if you begin to have haters come out of the shadows. This may be inevitable. As long as you are doing your best and taking care of those you supervise, go ahead and ignore them.

Awards: The Biggest Scam in the Air Force

I'm not saying that to scare you. I say it for a reason, a good one. Over the years I have noticed something everyone else has. Something right under our nose. We all see it, and although it happens right in front of us, we still react the same way we did the first time we saw The Sixth Sense. Damn! The whole time?!

What I'm talking about is the biggest scam in the Air Force, and it unfortunately impacts careers. Maybe I shouldn't use the word scam, but how else can you describe the awards system? This system, more definitively, this process is, at its core, well intended. But when you add people to it, the whole thing gets extremely inflated.

The awards system is full of fluff, and everyone knows it yet does nothing (at least mentionable) to stop it. The sad truth is that, if you are a solid worker—let's say a staff sergeant who does their job and does it well, is out in the community, leading that private organization and also concerned with education, taking a class a quarter—you cannot win with truth. You cannot simply put the truth on a 1206 and win. It doesn't work that way. Don't believe me? Try it. If you are reading this book and can go through all your winning packages and say that nothing is inflated, embellished, or otherwise, you are a true saint.

Sitting at the group allowed me to see all those badass packages every quarter and annually. Being the guy on the base who is responsible for capturing all the savings throughout the wing, I was excited to take a gander and throw two fists in the air when I felt giddy with excitement. Peering at that first 1206, I wasn't let down! Oh, wow, it says, "saved AF $10M." This is *huge*! Wait, another one, two lines down reads, "22K man-hours back to unit." Holy crap, I'm in heaven! These people are changing the game on their own!

When I went through the first set of packages, 21 of them to be exact, I started to see a trend. After doing some quick math, these

Mission Support Group packages alone collectively saved the Air Force $330M and 220K man-hours. That was more than the whole wing budget!

Wait. Why haven't these people captured these savings? I must not be doing my job. I then did something that really opened my eyes. I had an awakening of sorts.

My boss gave me the green light to send the bullets to the superintendents and flight chiefs of the squadron where the bullet originated. My email spelled out I was in no way trying to validate the bullets, just trying to capture them so the wing received credit for the savings in accordance with the Innovation and Transformation Office (IAW) business rules. Click. Sent.

After a couple days of crickets, I made a few calls to the people I look up to, people who would get Air Force tattoos on the side of their neck if it were within regulations. More crickets. And then even more crickets.

Not one bullet ended up being captured. About 90 percent of them were fluffed up beyond belief. In fact, the airman who won the annual award had saved $2M by preventing a rapid runway closure, yet when I talked to their boss, I found out the guy assisted a team that was TDY with a U-Drive-It car from LRS (logistics readiness squadron). Had he not done this, they would not have had a car, therefore not been able to do the runway survey, therefore the runway would have closed (or they would have simply rented a vehicle on their own). This is bullshit, and yet no one seemed to have caught it. Or is it okay to play Six Degrees of Kevin Bacon?

To further illustrate, I decided to see how our first core value stood up against this system. I wrote a quarterly package and jacked up the numbers enormously. Not one person asked a question, and it almost won at the wing. Taking someone at their word is great—until it isn't.

This secret process is right under our noses and we all know it. Some navigate the head winds and, with a supervision's help, get up a fluffed package. The question has to be asked, "If it is broke, how can we fix it?" As I like to say in my green belt classes, "If you can't measure it, you can't fix it." We simply don't know what is true and what isn't. A feeble attempt at sending out the packages to another base and our base grading theirs was swiftly cut down. In this world of awards, you have to break this glass ceiling and fight with integrity, credibility, and persistence. You know it is a horrific process, but you cannot give up, because there are too many implications attached. The fact remains that awards win awards—and promote people.

So you ask if this broken system is how people get promoted.

Not really. I'm saying awards play a significant role in promotion, and we all need to speak up about their integrity. Is it right that the names are right in front of the board? At a small base, you are basically grading your friend's, colleague's, or an acquaintance's package. This is a severe disadvantage for you introverts out there.

I can't pretend to have the answer to this crisis. I know there are outstanding leaders out there, working on putting control measures in place to keep some of this fragmented integrity intact. It's starting to go the right way when they stipulate you cannot grade your own member's package and they mask the names on EPRs for the people under consideration. In the meantime, the true north on your compass is to apply for awards and to time them when your chances are best. You need to be relentless in doing everything with excellence and truthfully capturing it on paper. Do not wait until the last minute. The second you find out that punk from FSS (force support squadron) beat you, start working on your game plan and get your supervisor involved as you plot out the next attack. If you get off the train, it will stop, backup, and run your ass over.

I hope the above rant sheds a little light on this problem and that we, as a body, somehow find ways to allow hard-working staff sergeants a chance through truthful evaluation. If not, we will continue to promote and recognize people who are just as good, only they can write better. That, my friends, is not cool.

Chapter 4

Maximize Your Time

Living Out What Is Inside

"Most of us have two lives. The life we live, and the unlived life within us. Between the two stands Resistance." —Steven Pressfield

One of the books that changed the way I look at things is *The War of Art* by Steven Pressfield. This cognitive kick in the ass set me straight and, no shit, allowed me to finish writing this book. Why is Pressfield's book so good? Because it pokes, prods, and stabs that wound we all live with. That feeling inside us that says we are more than where we are, more than who we are. We all have something inside us that is on fire, and we find ways to let resistance win so we never truly do what it is we want to do, namely, what makes us happy. Instead, we continue heading to work, making the commander's call, shuffling through hordes of emails, and waiting for Friday to come. Resistance, Pressfield pointed out, "is the most toxic thing in the universe and it is a real bitch to get away from."

Why is it when someone is told they have some crazy illness that will kill them within six months, they immediately quit their job and pursue their dreams? It reminds me of that movie with Jack Nicholson, "The Bucket List." These two old guys are about to die, so they do all the things they always wanted to do. What the hell? Why didn't they do it all in the first place? How come we let life kick us in the balls instead of taking that bull by the horns? If you want to jump out of a plane, do it. If you want to be a hard-nosed Wall Street broker, do it. If you want to write a book about being successful as an enlisted member of the armed forces, do it! Those old guys should teach us all that time is truly finite, and it will pass us up without regard for how we feel about it.

Pressfield is one of the only authors who got me standing up while holding a book. Using his unparalleled words, this is Resistance:

- **Resistance is invisible:** It cannot be seen, heard, or smelled. But there is a force. This force's aim is to distract us.

- **Resistance is internal:** No one but you manifests Resistance. No one else.

- **Resistance is insidious:** It will take any form to deceive you. It will do whatever it takes to keep you from doing your work. It has no conscience. It will double-cross you the second your back is turned. Resistance is always lying and full of shit.

- **Resistance is implacable**: You cannot reason with it, just as you cannot reason with Jaws or a Terminator. It does not fatigue. Reduce it to a single cell, and that cell will attack you.

- **Resistance is impersonal:** It doesn't care who you are. It just doesn't like you. Resistance is a true force of nature. It acts objectively.

Everyone feels resistance!

- **Resistance plays for keeps:** Its goal isn't to wound or disable. Resistance aims to kill. It targets your soul. It wants to destroy that unique and priceless gift we were put on this earth to give. Resistance means business.

"We feed resistance with power by our fear of it. Master the fear and we conquer resistance." — Steven Pressfield

The thing is, we all procrastinate. It isn't something only you are doing. We all do it each and every day. We know we want to get promoted, but are we studying enough to make it happen? If you have ever written down your goals, which I recommend, you will undoubtedly look back and see you may or may not have reached them. I was going through my goals from 2014, and since then, I have met about 60 percent of them. How can this be? The disheartening feeling of looking at that unchecked box, knowing you had enough time to complete the goal in front of you. So why didn't you? There are 168 hours in a week. Even with work and sleep, there is so much time to do whatever you truly want to do. Why let resistance win? The toxicity is real and if you don't do something *right now*, you may never do anything. You may end up very average, a statistic of someone who had something special and never dug his or her heels in to make it happen. Settling for what society wants. Everyone loves average. I have never met anyone who doesn't love average. It is when you separate yourself from the pack, when you follow your dreams and beat resistance that people start to act differently toward you. "You've changed, man." Yes, I know. I kicked Resistance's ass.

Cut the Nonsense

> *"Emails are straight up time-killers."*
> — A. J. Kehl

Ensuring we are not wasting our time in this world on a million things pulling us in a billion different directions is no easy task. I can't tell you how many times I have had a mental hernia trying to stop time and not feeling like I have done anything productive. Have you ever had that kind of day? The kind where thousands of things happen, but then, once close of business hits, you feel like nothing *actually* was accomplished? This is how almost all of my days went for a long time. Sure, things were happening, but I knew deep down I was not using my time in the most effective way. I would sit and write down ideas on my whiteboard, hoping to crack the damned Da Vinci code of time in the workplace. Finally, after days of finding a good target to bang my head against and reading some Tim Ferriss (pretty awesome author), I found a few ways to manage my time more wisely. I'd like to share these tricks with you.

Don't trip out when I tell you what these are. They may sound impossible at first, but they work. Trust me! This has become policy in my life. No room for movement. My time and, more important, *your time* depend on it.

1. Only check your email twice a day. I always get immediate reactions on this one because we live and die by email. It is right up there with our cell phones and oxygen in terms of needs. But you don't really need to check your email more often. Why? Because you will quickly find that nothing is really dropped if you are strategic about what times to read them. Go for something like 1100 and 1600. These times are critical because, as I said in an earlier chapter, you want to knock out your most important tasks early in the day. *Do not* check your email first thing in the morning or you will find yourself diving into 100 nonsense emails and three cups of that muddy office coffee you keep brewing (get a French press already!).

2. Make email your auto-friend. What I mean by this is, first, turn off your little pop-up feature that tells you when an email comes in. I, like you, have mad ADHD and I can't help but read the damned thing when it shows up on my screen. You know what, just close Outlook altogether. Second, you want to have an auto-response email ready to roll so people know you mean business. I have a hard time keeping this up and surely need to take my own advice. In the auto-response, indicate you check emails twice a day and at what times. If something is truly an emergency, they can call your cell (and leave your cell number). End it with something like, "Thank you for understanding. This process allows me to better serve you." I'm telling you, this will really open some "make time" in your day.

3. Create a "make time" schedule. The majority of your impactful work typically happens on Monday and Tuesday. You are fresh off the weekend and eager to dominate. Creating a "make time" schedule is all about focusing on the times you should be your most productive. These are the times where you close Outlook, shut the door, and ignore phone calls. This is about impact. I allot time at the beginning of the week for my larger projects. Midweek there are some blocked times for smaller rocks, but still, I need the time. By Friday most are ready for the weekend, and your productivity will likely suffer. For this reason I like to schedule my relationship-building time at the end of the week.

This is when I focus on going around and talking to people. It, too, is impactful!

4. Try to avoid meetings at all costs. Want the truth? *You can't handle the truth!* Just kidding. The truth is, meetings are usually a waste of time. I will get to that mess in a moment, but first, for the sake of time, let me cut to the chase: an email can usually solve a question or issue quicker than a meeting. Try to solve whatever issue or question via email first, then phone, then, finally, a meeting. When you respond to an email, be concise. When you draft an email, be clear and to the point. Both are equally important so no time is wasted on irrelevant topics.

Curbing Death by PowerPoint

Look, I'm just like you. If I want a severe case of the "itis," all I need to do is listen to 99 percent of the PowerPoint presentations force-fed to us daily in the Air Force. The fact is, PowerPoint is only boring because people are either lazy or they don't know what they are doing. Whatever the reason, we need to find a way to not kill our audience with boredom the next time we deliver a brief.

I recently went through another (yes, another) professional development seminar and there had to have been 25 deathly briefings. But the 26th brief stood out. It wasn't like the rest. It wasn't another sorry template with a crowded slide of bullet points, depressing you more than that time your team missed the chip-shot field goal to lose the Super Bowl in overtime. No, this thing was awesome! How the hell can a PowerPoint be awesome? Glad you asked. Here are five ways that one was badass and how yours can be too.

1. Use solid colors to make it pop. A strong palette of solid colors can make for an awesome presentation. Enough with the cliché templates too. We have all seen them. Let it go.

2. Stop using PowerPoint! Seriously, you should try other programs that are way cooler, like Prezi, which will make you stand out instantly. Check out Prezi at https://prezi.com.

3. Use an awesome font and leave the other words on the slide in a regular font. This allows everything to stand out. Oh, and for the love of God, don't put more than 10 words on one slide. No one wants to read all that stuff.

4. Photos are key. This doesn't mean you *have* to use photos. But if you do, make sure they are professional images. I don't want to be reminded that everything in the 1990s was pixilated.

5. If it is boring stuff, throw in some randomness. Admit it sucks and crack a few jokes. Get on audience's level and they will appreciate what you have to say much more.

PowerPoint sucks, but using the tips above can alleviate the excruciating pain we all endure when we have to sit through one. Make yours different. The 26th brief I told you about used Prezi, which is compatible with PowerPoint, and it was pretty awesome!

A Quick Jab at Meetings

"Meetings are an addictive, highly self-indulgent activity that corporations and other organizations habitually engage in only because they cannot actually masturbate." — Dave Barry

Meetings are the time you sit around and talk about all the things you should be doing. If you want to maximize your time in a meeting, keep it short. The most important thing that should come out of *all* meetings is action. Everyone should have to take action on something. Don't just sit around and BS. The second-most-important thing you can do, if it is your meeting anyway, is keep it on time with an established agenda. This is critical.

Want to make it interesting? Steve Jobs used to have walking meetings. Put that running track to use outside of the PT test!

First thing you should do if you are a manager is ask yourself if the meeting is worth having. If it is, then reduce the number of attendees. This saves time, because the meeting will end sooner, and those who don't attend can do other, more productive things. If the meeting needs to happen, here are a few tips to make it more productive:

- Start on time: If it is a 1500 meeting, don't waste time. Time is a finite resource!
- Don't recap for late people: You are basically starting the meeting over at that point.
- Publicize the agenda: This way, people can prepare. That should be another bullet: Be prepared!
- Document your meeting with action items for the people involved: How often do we go to the next meeting and jaw about the same things that were supposedly covered.

The Importance of Punctuality

Is it me or has society quietly written off punctuality? Am I the only one who simply cannot stand tardiness, regardless of who you are or your rank? Please say it isn't so.

Being tardy shows a serious lack of respect. It tells the other person their time isn't as valuable as yours, and believe me, that's going to stick in their mind for quite some time. It also insults their intelligence when you make some random excuse like, "Traffic at the gate was crazy" or "I had to take my kids to the CDC." How are those excuses? Simply put, they aren't.

It's kind of funny, in the military there is a common notion that if you are on time you are already 15 minutes late. The hurry-up-and-wait routine is a dance I've danced many times! But the metrology behind the 15-minute adage is totally legit. Being early allows you to have small miscues and still be on time.

Tardiness in the Air Force is quite common, unfortunately, and I want to lay a few things out to show you the importance of timeliness:

1. Is it ever acceptable? Yes. Look, shit happens. There are unavoidable things that happen that sometimes make us late. But let's say it's something like your alarm doesn't go off. Okay, well if you don't set an additional alarm from that point on, you have no leg to stand on. The key point here is that, as supervisors, we can't put anyone in a guillotine if they are late one time. I talked with a SNCO a year or two ago when I was new to the

Spangdahlem Fire Department. He explained if I were to be late for work, it was an automatic LOR (letter of reprimand). What!? There are big implications for that. This might happen to the best, most credible member, and you'll fry them that quickly? I think that's poor leadership.

2. Time is money, short and simple. We have a mission to do, and if you're late, that hurts the mission in one way or another. Tardiness is a symptom of discipline. If you can't be relied on to be on time, how can your team rely on you in the field?

3. Rank has nothing to do with it. I don't care if you outrank me, if you are late to a class I'm teaching or a meeting I'm facilitating, I will remember. Frankly, you're being rude. We must all value our time and make it clear to others that punctuality holds high value as well. To be fair, I'm not perfect, but I know the importance of being on time.

In the end, we are all late from time to time. But being tardy simple isn't worth the potential domino effect. All we can do is understand its importance in our lives and make it a point to be on time.

From a cultural perspective, punctuality is either really, really important or not a huge deal, depending on where you are, what country or region you're in. For instance, Pacific Islanders have a laid-back life. They don't view time as we do in the United States. It is an afterthought. If you're scheduled to meet at the beach at 5:00 p.m. for a barbecue, it's totally acceptable to get there a little later. On the flip side, in Germany, being punctual is woven into the fabric of common politeness. It is considered very rude to show up after a predetermined time.

Old Uncle Outsource

"If you chop three zeros off of your income and half it, that's roughly your hourly income (assuming 40 hours per week average and two weeks of vacation per year). So, if you make $50,000 per year, you make approximately $25 per hour. For far less than that, you will be able to out-source nearly anything in your life that you dislike."
— Tim Ferriss

Ah, outsourcing. You're reading this and wondering why the hell it's in this book. Well, it belongs here because my goal is to hook you up with all the ways you can maximize your enlistment, and outsourcing, that is, paying someone else to do those things you either dread doing or you simply don't have time to do is one of the ways you can do everything. Yes, it is legal, and yes, it is a huge opportunity to make things happen without, you know, making things happen. Civilians outsource all sorts of crazy things like managing emails (Zirtual, www.zirtual.com), doing laundry (FlyCleaners, http://flycleaners.com) marketing their product or service, developing podcasts, running personal errands (Handy, www.handy.com), and even household chores (don't tell your dependent, as they may find a way to get out of that). The fact is, outsourcing is huge. If you don't believe me, just look at Uber, the ride-sharing company that has changed the way we get around. Outsourcing has helped so many people in so many ways. So why can't it help us?

Outsourcing can directly impact your overall time effectiveness and help you truly maximize your enlistment. My three main sources are:

- Your Man in India https://yourmaninindia.com: This is the secret weapon. A freaking virtual assistant.
- Hello Alfred www.helloalfred.com: Shopping.
- TaskRabbit www.taskrabbit.com: Obviously for tasks.

Although I have messed around with a few others, these are the ones that have actually produced tangible results for me. When I'm working on a big project that is due soon and has high value to the organization, I ask Hello Alfred to buy those flowers for my girl and have them delivered to her. When I have small tasks to do that interfere with my Q2 time (more on Q2 on next page,) I hit up TaskRabbit to make it happen. When I need a virtual assistant to do some real work for me, Your Man in India makes that dream a reality. For instance, let's say you want to write some articles for a publication in your field, but sometimes you don't have the time to write them. YMII makes it happen. This is important because writing gigs usually pay out, so if you're paying someone $20 to write a piece that a magazine publisher will pay you $50 for, you are netting $30 for doing next to nothing!

Here is a quick disclaimer to keep my ass out of trouble. I do not endorse the following as it is simply something out there. If you choose to utilize it if you want. Okay, now that the lame part is over, let me tell you what I mean.

With online school making up a vast majority of colleges this day in age, it is easy to attend school from anywhere in the world. You could be drinking a San Miguel Light in the Philippines on the beach and attend class—as long as you have Wi-Fi. What if you have a homework assignment but would rather play beach volleyball? What are you going to do? Email Your Man in India, which is simply a well-educated person whose life goal at that moment is to ensure your satisfaction, and send it to them to do. For a *very* small price, this educated (often graduate-level) person will write that puppy better than you can! Yes, this is real, and it's a viable option. Too good to be true, isn't it.

Now, like I said, I do not recommend that, but in an Air Force where education is playing a higher and higher role, some people may need this service from time to time. I still believe that obtaining your own education is the best way to mentally grow. It is up to you what you do with this information. Whatever you decide, do not use your TA to do this or you will be in big trouble mister.

Do yourself a favor and take a look at all the outsourcing opportunities that are out there and find out for yourself what works for you. Who knows, it may help you along your journey. You're welcome.

MRU Tip
Master your strengths—outsource your weaknesses.

The Four Quadrants of Your Time

> *"Time = LIFE. Therefore, waste your time and waste your life.*
> *Master your time and master your life."* — Alan Lakein

Why am I talking so much about time? In today's world, that seems to be the loudest gripe coming out of our hardworking members. Time is elusive and finite. We often find ourselves putting out so many spot fires that the seat of the fire never gets any attention. What I mean is we aren't taking time to handle those tasks or projects that are most important. This is because every two seconds we hear that little noise Outlook makes when an email comes in. All day, constant, pointless emails. The important ones get buried in the bullshit.

Time should be looked at as one of the most important elements of management. We are all wired to multitask everything, even though the majority of us know that that is *dead wrong*. Time and time again, research shows when we put all of our focus on one thing, we are substantially more effective than if we multitask. To be frank, multitasking is a waste of your valuable time.

One day, while driving to Austria, I decided to listen to a podcast to kill the time (I often listen to audiobooks during long drives to ensure I'm constantly developing). This one was all about time and how bad we suck at it. As I listened, passing through the northern Alps, I started to figure out a way I could pull out the information that would apply to those of us in the military. I wanted to create a simple yet effective way to use the podcaster's foundation and make it into something we could put into use tomorrow. Here is a look at the four quadrants of your time as publicized by the great Stephen Covey:

- **Q1: Urgent and Important.** Freaking Q1. We don't really want to be in this quadrant. How many times have you been working on something and your boss drops something else on your head that he deems more important? Probably often. Q1 is something that has to be done in the next 24 hours and has high importance. By high importance, I mean important to the business or leadership, and if you don't do it, there will be serious repercussions to the mission or you. Freaking Q1!

- **Q2: Not Urgent but Important.** Ahh. Q2 is the sweet spot. This is where you want to be as much as possible. These are the projects or tasks that are due in the next week or so, and you are being proactive, tackling the big stuff early. Q2 will change your life. Doesn't it make sense to complete the things that have the most significance, the items that make the biggest difference? It sure does. Q2, baby! Q2!

- **Q3: Urgent but Not Important.** Q3 is a necessity, although we don't like it. Those above you deem some things urgent, but they really have no significance in your mission. These are things like, "We have a mandatory blah blah blah in an hour." Here you are dominating Q2 tasks, and now you have to stop that in order to do this Q3 stuff. I'm thinking about a vast majority of computer-based training (CBTs), some commander's (CC) calls, and a redundant report due to leadership.

- **Q4: Not Urgent and Not Important.** Q4 is where many people like to hang out. I see Q4 happening all around me and I just don't get it. Sure, you need to find time to sit around in your underwear and watch Dexter or Saved by the Bell reruns. But this should be limited. Q4 is playing video games and procrastinating about those items that are currently Q2 eligible but will become Q1 the more you sit on the couch. Get what I mean? Q4 is a must, albeit a limited must.

To make sure you are in Q2 as much as possible, I'm sharing with you a way you can set up your Outlook to bring the Q2 upfront and eliminate the unimportant stuff from your view. I have had my email like this for about a year now, and it has truly made a difference.

Are you in control of your in-box? Do you often see "mailbox full"? Ever work hard all day only to go home and feel like nothing was accomplished? Are you multitasking? If so, you are hurting yourself. Email is a disruption to our "make time." Here is a way you can stop the bleeding and focus on Q2:

1. Change the way you manage your emails by clicking on the arrow in the lower right corner of the Quick Steps panel at the top of the screen.

2. The different actions you will use include Move to Folder, Flag, and Categorize.

3. The only three folders you need are (1) Action, (2) Read, and (3) Archive (by conversation). These will be new .pst folders, and

when you click Quick Step, the program will automatically file your email where you want it to go.

4. The Action folder will have a Quick Step for the following: Action–Urgent (within 24 hours), Action–When possible (not immediate), and Action–Waiting on Response (actionable after receiving a response).

With this setup, you can easily and quickly filter the contents of your in-box, allowing you to focus on what is most important. This will get rid of all the crap that distracts you from what's valuable. Here are a few tips for going through your emails with this simple setup:

1. Be sure to use the reading pane as you filter.

2. Reply to sender during an email check only if it will take two minutes or less.

3. Set your Start option to open Outlook to your Action folder (File-Options-Advanced-Set to Open).

4. Use the 4 Ds:
   • Delete it.
   • Do it.
   • Delegate it.
   • Defer it.

Understanding how finite time is will ensure you pay closer attention.

Having a system will ensure success and allow you to focus on impact.

The four quadrants of time are something that really changed my productivity levels, and I believe the same will happen for you.

Give it a try!

Focus on Q2, baby!

Chapter 5

Leveraging Military Finances

Start Building Young

"Procrastination is the grave in which opportunity is buried."
— Unknown

I'm not wealthy. I have a long way to go to reach my goals.

But I do have things lined up, and while I'm not a credentialed financial advisor, I can offer you some advice on how to invest even when Uncle Sam is paying you modestly. One of the best pieces of advice I received was to start early to build wealth. I was 18 years old, and my pops told me I should save some money—no shit. I decided to go with a Roth IRA (more on that later), and that was my very first investment. Over time that money, through what's dollar cost averaging, has compounded and grown into a nice heap of cash. The earlier you start to save your money, the better. In fact, one year can make a gigantic difference! If I were to show you a graph of this, it would look like the ascent of Mount Fuji, slowly rising above the clouds and then a steep climb to the top.

Many may not see how a little bit of savings helps over time. I know I didn't. That was, until I read The Automatic Millionaire by David Bach. He showed me the importance of using the things we may spend on every day to create a long-term savings plan. This was dubbed "The Starbucks Rule." Put briefly, many people spend an average of $5.00 a day on Starbucks. (I'm pretty sure that number is edging closer to $10.00.) If not spent on coffee, that $5.00 could be used to produce some pretty nice results. Using a daily equation, if you did this five times a week, it would come out to $1,300 for the year. That isn't bad. How about if you earned 5% on that? That's another $65.00 a year. 10% is $130/year! Over a 20-year period, you could save and earn (interest) about $31,000 just by brewing your own coffee! This basic elementary principle should be applied at an early age because of the magic of compounding interest.

MRU Tip
The most basic principle of investing is use *time* to your advantage.

The Starbucks Rule aside, you need to be doing something and doing it early. The key is to pay yourself *before* you pay anything else. How does this work? Basically, set up automatic allotments into some areas that will make you wealthier before you pay your bills (money to others). This concept seems twisted at first, but it is real and an absolute must to get financially healthy. Hell, with many retirement accounts, you can even pay yourself before taxes—now that's putting yourself on the right track. So what will you do to pay yourself first? How will you smile in satisfaction that your nest egg is growing before a frown appears in the form of paying those damned cell phone, car, and utility bills?

When you are young and you get a true understanding of finances, you can leverage your mediocre pay into something substantial. This starts with paying yourself first, but there is a key rule you have to follow. This rule, tested by many and ruining the majority, is one that cannot be argued with. If you follow this rule, you have a chance to make it financially and build true wealth before that 20-year pension plan kicks in. You ready?

Do not freaking buy a new, expensive car.

Time and time again, young airmen with no real financial foundation get that sweet new ride. This mistake often leads you down a road of paying others and not yourself. Hang in there with a beater car for a few years as you build your savings. In the end, if you absolutely want to buy a new car, get one that's at least two years old and make sure you are investing (notice I didn't say saving) at least 15 percent of your gross income (your income before taxes). Around two years old is the sweet spot when it comes to a car's value versus depreciation.

TSP 101: Traditional vs. Roth

With the Roth Thrift Savings Plan (TSP) now available, people are scratching their heads and wondering where the heck to put their money. To make it more complicated, the traditional TSP is based on a percentage of your gross income, whereas the Roth option is a set monetary value. So which one is better? Well, I'm definitely not a financial advisor, but as a 10-year TSP participant and a guy who prides himself on learning what he can about finances, I feel I can at least throw out the difference between the two and my opinion as to which is the way to go. Keep in mind we will have another sweet tidbit on which funds to invest in. Let's take a look at which route to go: traditional or Roth.

First, let's look at the traditional TSP. Because you fund your TSP with pretax dollars, you actually lower the amount of income you must pay taxes on. This, in turn, decreases your tax burden while you're employed, which can be particularly significant if you contribute the maximum amount or are in a high income tax bracket.

Pretty simple, right? A good tip is to start with a comfortable percentage of your gross income (pretax) and then gradually increase it over time. I increase my withholding 2 percent for promotion and 1 percent for every two-year bump in pay. This keeps me in line, living within my means.

Now, let's look at the Roth. Unlike the traditional TSP, the Roth alternative allows investors to contribute after-tax income to the fund. As a result, all withdrawals upon retirement are completely tax free. That's right, I said tax free. To me, this is the winner. I prefer the Roth because I simply don't know what tax bracket I will be in when I'm super old. But I do know exactly what I will be taxed as I make my contributions now. Maybe I'm just optimistic, but I would like to think I will be successful and therefore in a higher bracket later in life. Why would I want to take that chance?

Both plans are pretty awesome, mainly because the expense ratios are one of the lowest available. But if I had to make a choice between the two, I would choose the Roth option.

As of this writing, I contribute 10 percent to the traditional TSP and $200 a month to the Roth. Life happens, so things change. One final though to mention is that the new blended retirement plan is in full effect. For folks entering active duty nowadays, you are automatically enrolled in the TSP and now the government will match contributions! The government will begin matching at 1% while you are contributing 3%. After two years of service, the government will match the member's contributions up to an additional 4%. Basically, you want to maximize this because if you contribute 5%, the government will throw another 5% on top of it. What a deal.

TSP 101: Taxes and Withdrawals

Because the TSP is a deferred plan, you will pay taxes on your contributions and their growth, either now or later, but you will not be taxed until you start to withdraw funds during retirement, which is defined as over the age of 59½ (compare that to some other countries if you think that's too old).

If you withdraw funds prior to this age, you will be required to pay a 10 percent penalty tax plus regular income tax on the entire amount withdrawn—with one exception.

With the TSP, you have the option of early retirement (bet you didn't know that). Specifically, if you retire or otherwise separate from service at or after age 55 but before age 59½, you can withdraw funds from your TSP without paying the 10 percent early withdrawal penalty. But you will still be subject to regular income tax, as you would with any withdrawals. But, hey, what can you do?

Do you know how cheap the TSP is? The TSP charges an annual expense ratio of just 0.038 percent of assets (whereas annual fees and expenses for 401[k] plans range, on average, between 1 and 2 percent).

The TSP lets you choose one of five index mutual funds or a target-date fund, which automatically becomes more conservative as your retirement date gets closer. As of 2017, you can invest up to $18,000 annually in the TSP, and if you're receiving tax-free income while deployed, you can boost your contributions to $54,000 for the year. And now you have access to a Roth TSP too, which is like a Roth IRA, but without the income restrictions.

Maximizing your TSP is smart because your money is sheltered from your taxable income. Putting your money in the stock market is by far the best financial decision you can make with your enlisted pay.

My Rich Uncle recommends the FANG stocks (Facebook, Amazon, Netflix, and Google), along with a steady income earner like Realty Income or Crown Castle Income. Monthly dividends over 4.5 percent? Yes, please!

Maximize Your Investing Power

Another important piece of the financial puzzle is to learn about investing immediately. When you know that time is your greatest ally, learning about things like stocks, bonds, real estate, and other market investments arms you with the knowledge to make sound decisions while managing risk. In school, all they tell you is to save money. They don't really get into how it all works and how you can benefit from it. The market is volatile at times, yes, but it is the single greatest way to leverage Uncle Sam's money.

As a beginner, start looking at some financial websites, like *Yahoo! Finance*, and reading books like *Investing for Dummies*. Once you have a working knowledge of the power of investing, open an online brokerage account so you can get in on the action. An online brokerage account is simply a savings account where the brokerage firm brokers the deal for you to be able to own a position (amount of stock). This is known as equity investing.

- Capital One ShareBuilder: I have been with Capital One ShareBuilder since the beginning. They have a plan in which you pay $12 a month and they broker up to six trades (money into stock[s] of your choosing). This is a simple platform and single trades cost $9.95.

- E*Trade: This is an online broker that offers lots of useful information and tools on how to analyze different stocks, receive analyst recommendations, etc. It is also $9.95 a trade.

- TD Ameritrade: If you want to do it all and have all the tools to really go in-depth, this is the site to use. It is around the same cost per trade as the others, but this is a more advanced platform.

Once you have an online brokerage account set up, you are already doing something the majority of your peers are missing. When I was young and didn't have much money to invest, I set up the automatic investment feature from ShareBuilder and simply put money here and there. I was able to throw $200 a month into four stocks, all for a $12 fee. Not too bad!

Add Stocks to your Life

Many people seem to be afraid of stocks. They think it's too risky. The majority of these Negative Nancies are simply uninformed. When you are ignorant, you tend to be more negative about something. But it really sucks for them because they are missing out on a huge opportunity. Stocks come with risk, as does any investment, but they aren't as bad as you think, and the upside can be tremendous. At twenty-something years old, if I can put $1,000 into something with a chance of it growing significantly, I'm going to do that. If it doesn't pan out, I'm only a twenty-something!

I still remember sitting in a dayroom-kitchen area with a buddy, learning about this stock market stuff. He and I were reading up on stocks and opened our own brokerage accounts. We were stoked! We each had $1,000 and wanted to put it toward something. To this day, I wish I had followed his position as he argued that a company named Google seemed like a good investment. This was 2006 and Google was already a household name, but no one really knew its financial capabilities. I argued, "No way. Nutrisystem is the spot." Nutrisystem is a trendy weight-loss, ready-to-eat meal company. To this day, he still has his position in Google, and as you might guess, it has grown to be quite an investment. Meanwhile, Nutrisystem failed over the long term. This was when I learned lesson number one about beginner's investing: Go with what you know.

- "Just Google it."
- "Netflix and chill."
- "I will Facebook you."
- "Bro, Amazon it."
- "Got my iPhone upgrade."

Notice a trend? If there is a saying for a company or it is embedded into everyday culture, it is probably worth looking into. If you invested in any of these companies at *any* point in the last 10 years and held on to it, you would have made some serious money. In fact, $1,000 in Amazon when it first went public (called an IPO or initial public offering) would have you now sitting with $491,000 in your pocket. No joke!

I always have 50% or more of my investments in stocks. More than anything else, stocks are the quickest, most efficient way to grow a modest paycheck into a respectable asset. Add in some dividend-paying stocks (companies that pay you cash monthly, quarterly, or annually), and you could even have supplemental income! Companies like the Realty Income, a real estate investment trust (REIT) with the ticker symbol O, pays out a monthly dividend!

I repeat, I'm not a financial advisor. I'm simply showing you some ways to maximize your enlistment. If you are like me, you want to build long-term wealth. I had no idea what I was doing, but I made it a hobby to learn all I could. At the end of the day, putting money in a savings account that doesn't grow is simply not an intelligent way to save. Why not put it somewhere it grows *for you?* Not ready to jump into individual stocks? Simply invest in an index fund and treat it like a savings account. It will grow over time. You owe it to yourself to pay *yourself* first and to learn how to grow that money so, when that uniform comes off, you are not codependent on the military for money.

Frugal Living Equals Long-Term Wealth

"It's not your salary that makes you rich, it's your spending habits."
— Charles A. Jaffe

If you joined the enlisted force to make money, you chose poorly. Whether it is for a higher calling or to proudly serve your country, joining the military is a choice we make for nonmonetary rewards. For me, it was a way out of where I lived and a chance to see the world. Couple that with a free education that, at the time, my family couldn't afford for me, and I enrolled in MEPS (military entrance processing station) quickly! Why did you join? Is there a specific reason?

Although money isn't galling off the trees here in the enlisted force, that doesn't mean you can't eventually make enough to allow you a little freedom to build wealth. Other than promotion, most of the questions I field are about finances and how to build a foundation of wealth, even on a paycheck that only allows us to stay at Holiday Inns. Military money is still money that can be manipulated, and it can grow with some knowledge fertilizer.

I knew a senior airman named Dan with savings of almost $100K. If you are in your twenties, that kind of money saved and easily liquidated is pretty damned good. Dan accomplished this by living below his means, that is, below what he could afford if he chose to. Dan didn't have flashy clothes or shiny cars. He made most of his meals at home, bought what he could in bulk, traveled modestly, and saved a set amount of every paycheck. Unlike Dan, most people fall into the old "big hat, no cattle" routine. They have the coolest gadgets, a new BMW, and eat out basically every day. The problem is that 90 percent of the time their savings account looks as barren as the ruins of Chernobyl.

Dan did what we are told to do: He lived on less than his paycheck and he saved. I call this "shoebox savings," and although it can work, it is a legacy process that will only build true wealth if you live like a homeless person. If you're like me, you probably want to have some freedom to travel, eat out with friends, and live free in the military, especially if you are stationed overseas! There are a bunch of ways you can set yourself up to amass superior wealth to Dan's while still living out a dream.

Is the Savings Deposit Program Worth It?

At lot of us know about this sweet deal. Go to a combat zone for at least 30 days and you're eligible for a guaranteed 10 percent on every dollar saved during your deployment. Well, damn, sign me up!

Not so fast.

The Savings Deposit Program (SDP) sounds awesome, but there is definitely a catch that I have to disclose. The only money you can deposit into the SDP is money earned while in a deployed zone. It cannot be more than your monthly net pay. Why is this important? Well, the fact that one cannot just mic drop $10K and earn 10 percent in my opinion is an asterisk not well advertised. You don't need to be a math magician to see that 10 percent of $2,000 is less than 10 percent of $10,000. Plus 10 percent is an annual yield. If you are in the area for six months, depositing the maximum amount to the $10K limit and then continue for the allowed 90 days after your deployment, you would have been a part of the program for only 75 percent of the year. This means you will be cashing in 7.5 percent, not 10 percent. The last little catch to this smoke-and-mirror deal is that, although your pay isn't taxable in the combat zone, the government does take a rake to the interest earned on the SDP.

The key point here is that the SDP is a perk, not a financial opportunity. The most you can get is $1,000, and that's if you max it out. A regular bank would undoubtedly offer only 1 percent and that would land you $100 versus the SDP's $1,000. That $900 difference, or $2.50 a day, is not that awesome. But if you are in a combat zone and you don't need the money liquidated, why not grab a few extra bucks? It is very conservative but still something.

If you are like me, however, you want real financial opportunities. A few years ago I was going to setup a SDP, and then I found all these stipulations. So instead of setting the SDP up, I spent $9.95 to buy a bunch of GM stock (they were on the up-and-up) and netted 46 percent on my money. I'm not trying to give stock advice, but dang, that was a way better return on my cold hard cash! Bottom line: If you want to be ultraconservative, enter the SDP. If you want to actually make some real money, get into the stock market. It is only a matter of educating yourself.

BENEFIT ALERT! A financial advisor can cost you a pretty penny. Usually, it's a percentage of your investment, and at times it's a flat fee, often over $1,500. We have this service for *free*! Head down to the Airman and Family Readiness Center A&FRC and get sound advice from a certified, licensed financial advisor.

You Can Blow Your Deployment Money—I Don't

> *"Do not save what is left after saving, but spend what is left after saving."*
> — Warren Buffet

What do you do with your deployment money?

Do you buy a new PlayStation, go Amazon crazy, or purchase some other depreciating asset? I bet you do, and you are not alone. Most people do this, including myself. But a few years ago I made a switch that helped my deployment money grow for me, and you can too. See, becoming wealthy is all about your mind-set. The majority of people spend all their time trying to keep their head above water. They think poor. We must switch our mind-sets to think rich. Instead of working hard and then spending all that hard-earned money on some nice bauble that will depreciate overnight, why not think big? You can become rich, even on an enlisted military paycheck, if you think big. I can give no advice bigger than to be a homeowner. When you rent, you just burn money. You make someone else rich! When you own, you become a little wealthier with every month that passes. Believe it or not, owning is cheaper in the long run than renting. So what are you waiting for?

Every time you deploy, you get a chance to put away some money while focusing on your inner narcissist, working out constantly, and eating super healthy. That money you save adds up quickly and can be used to purchase a home. This purchase will bring you lasting income for years to come, whether you live in it or not. If you think you can't afford it, think again. Lenders will lend you money even if your credit is sketchy. Here are a few other reasons you should be a homeowner rather than a renter:

- **Homeowners get leverage.** This means you make money off of other people's money. In this case, your lender—who lets you borrow 80 percent or more of the purchase price—doesn't get to reap the profits. You do!

- **Homeowners get tax deductions.** This is huge. One of the most well-known tax deductions is mortgage interest. In short, the IRS lets you deduct all the interest you pay on your mortgage from your taxable income.

- **Homeowners can earn tax-free profits.** Yep. That wasn't a typo. Under current law, if you sell your primary residence (having lived in it for at least two of the last five years), you don't have to pay Uncle Sam taxes on the first $250,000 in profit.

- **If you rent out your house, you get a 1031 tax break.** The IRS won't tax you if your proceeds from a rental property sale go to another rental property.

If you are stationed overseas, you may think renting is your only option. Think again! Take the time to look into buying a home and letting your overseas housing allowance (OHA) pay your mortgage. In many areas, nearby bases will provide immediate renters for decades to come.

MRU Tip
If you don't want to go through a lender, you can always look for properties that are "owner will carry." The property owner becomes the lender and holds the note for a period of time. You don't have to mess with banks at all! One of my properties is this way, and it is working out amazingly well.

As military members, we all know what a sweet deal a VA loan is, right? This is a guaranteed loan that can really get you started on homeownership. Before you use it over any other available options, be sure to talk to a specialist. Here are some VA tidbits for you to chew on:

Four Reasons to Go with a VA Loan:

- No mortgage insurance premiums
- Guaranteed loan

- Beats national interest rates
- Special foreclosure protection for service members

MRU Tip

VA loans are awesome! But many people don't know they can be used for a variety of things.

VA Home Loans Can Be Used To:

- Buy a home or a condominium unit in a VA-approved project
- Build a home
- Simultaneously purchase and improve a home
- Improve a home by installing energy-saving features or making energy-efficient improvements
- Buy a manufactured home and/or lot

At the end of the day, you can be the guy who buys some new toys you can enjoy for a little while or you can buy something that will pay you back for years to come. Think big and think long term. Short-term thinking is for the people who want to remain stuck in their current situation. Even on a military paycheck, we can really build some financial freedom, and buying a home with your deployment money is an awesome decision. What a reward for your service!

Chapter 6

Milk Those Benefits!

Three Reasons to Milk Your Tuition Assistance

In October 2002, the military decided to increase tuition assistance (TA) from 75 percent to 100 percent. Hopping onto this Air Force train a year later, I have been fortunate to squeeze the juice out of that 100 percent to the best of my ability (although it still could be better). TA is awesome. Why? Each year the military gives you $4,500 to attend school. That's a nice chunk of change! But according to the RAND Corporation, only 15 percent of us are using this *free* money. What a shame! Here are three reasons you need to leverage your rich uncle:

1. **Money Talks:** You get up to $250 per semester hour, or the equivalent of the cost of college tuition, with a limit of $4,500 per fiscal year. Courses and degree programs may be academic or technical and can be taken at two-or four-year institutions on base, off base, or by correspondence. Now that's a deal, but that's not all. Did you know that many colleges reduce their rates for us? For example, Kaplan University's undergraduate tuition rate for service members, including the guard and the reserve, is reduced 55 percent to $165 per credit hour. Many other colleges follow suit, offering smokin' deals to those in uniform.

2. **Every State Is Your State**: Get this, no matter what state you are living in while on active duty, you will receive in-state tuition rates. If you don't think that is huge, you haven't crunched those

numbers! The National Center for Education Statistics (NCES) offers data to allow you to compare in-state and out-of-state tuitions. In 2012, the average tuition for an in-state undergraduate student at a four-year public school was $6,752. The average tuition for an out-of-state undergrad student at a four-year public school was $15,742. This means that, on average, it costs $8,990 more for students to attend a college or university in a state in which they are not a resident. I rest my case.

3. **The Great Incentive (GI) Bill:** As if it wasn't good enough, the Post-9/11 GI Bill is a reason alone to sign that dotted line. The benefits may be used for undergraduate and graduate degree programs, vocational and technical training, tutorial assistance, books, supplies, and monthly housing. Generally, benefits are payable for 15 years after release from active duty and may be transferred to spouses or dependent children. This is a big upgrade from the previous version because you have 15 years to use it (for 36 months) versus only 10 years with the old one. But, more important, you can transfer benefits to your kids or wife.

If you were to stay in the service for 20 years, that is over $91,000 in free money for education.

Educate Yourself, Fool!

"Education is the passport to the future,
for tomorrow belongs to those who prepare for it today."
— Malcolm X

Education in the Air Force is *free*. Why the hell would you not do something that is free and opens your mind?

When I look at the statistics, I see that only a fraction of the enlisted force actually uses this amazing benefit. But if you were to ask people, "Hey, why did you join the military?" a majority would include education in their answer. It is a great mystery why more people don't take advantage of this offer. Maybe it is the stress our people feel from their workload coupled with their home life, or maybe the fact that you have to work is revolting. What I know is the Air Force hooks up airmen with $4,500 a year in tuition assistance benefits. That isn't exactly a Harvard-level education, but if you are working on your CCAF (associate degree) or even an undergrad, that is plenty! In my experience, CCAF credits cost around $200 per credit hour. The annual allotment would get you through at least seven classes, and last time I checked (with the exception of your management credits, which you will get with Airman Leadership School), you only need five courses to dominate your CCAF. That's only one year and . . . boom! You have the educational requirement for senior master sergeant.

In today's highly educated enlisted force, we need to ensure we make time for this, because we can easily procrastinate. Ultimately, it will hurt us in more ways than one if we don't take advantage of that cash. So what's the formula? Well, I don't know.

In a recent Speed Mentoring held at Spangdahlem Air Base, I had a chance to talk to several SNCOs across the best wing in the Air Force (Spangdahlem AB won the Commander-in-Chief Excellence Award that year). I asked them, "Do you think the requirement will change from an associate's to a bachelor's degree for senior master sergeant?"

80 percent said no.
15 percent said "I think so."
5 percent said "It's possible."

This is a clear consensus. But then I asked, "Does a bachelor's degree look favorable on a master sergeant board?" Every single one of them said yes. You don't have to be a genius to see a degree can only help you as you climb this ladder.

The trick to making it happen is to pressure the hell out of yourself. Fortunately, my first supervisor made this a priority and held my EPR rating over my head, contingent on my educational progress. This was huge, but it's not very common, because most supervisors don't think about the impact of education those days.

My exact sequence goes like this:

Go to the Virtual Education Center on the AF Portal.
Apply for TA.

Ask yourself, "Why the hell would I do this? Now I *have* to take this class!"

Boom, you're on your way! Seriously, that is what I have done for years. The pressure forces you to move forward. It may seem dumb, but the truth is we all can make a million excuses why we don't have time for education. You will surprise yourself with how much time you will find when the money is on the line! For those of you who don't know, if you enroll in a class, using TA, you must pass that class with at least a C or you have to reimburse the TA out of your own pocket.

The Regional Versus National Debate

"Well, your school isn't regionally accredited, so it's no good." Have you heard that before? Yeah, me too. Although there is some validity to the fact a regionally accredited school is technically a better school in the long run, it doesn't mean that nationally accredited schools suck. So which will you go with? Well, it depends on your goals.

Let us first dive into what the hell difference there is between the two. Basically, the Department of Education must officially recognize the school to grant accreditation. This isn't an issue if you are in the military, because you can only use TA for accredited schools. Whether the school is regionally or nationally accredited depends on which accrediting educational association blesses them. These guys develop evaluation criteria and conduct peer evaluations to ensure schools meet established standards.

Regionally accredited schools typically hold higher standards in regard to academic rigor. Nationally accredited schools have high standards as well, but they also consider the type of delivery and can be specialty based. There is no arguing there are some major pros to a regionally accredited school, most notably the fact that 85 percent of schools are regionally accredited, so transferring and the prestige factor are not issues.

If you are set on attending a regionally accredited school so you don't have to sweat it later, be sure to visit the Department of Education website (https://www.ed.gov/accreditation) to confirm it is indeed regionally accredited.

Okay, so which do you go with? Like I said before, it totally depends on your long-term goals. If your plan is to do graduate work later and attempt to get out of the military and use it as leverage for a sweet job, you may want to consider regionally accredited schools. At the end of the day a nationally accredited school will surely take the credits from a regionally accredited school, but it's not always true the other way around!

Here comes the real deal.

Because *My Rich Uncle* is all about maximizing your enlistment, I'm going to give you the secret to this long debate, that is, as far as your military career goes.

It doesn't matter.

That's right. It simply doesn't matter when it comes to the military. Even if you were to apply to Officer Training School, the box on the application simply asks if you have an undergraduate degree. It doesn't ask about the school's accreditation. Moreover, when it comes to leveraging education for promotion, your career data brief, EPR, and SURF (single unit retrieval format) all simply ask if you have a degree and at what level. Accreditation is never mentioned. This is important because nationally accredited schools are easy to get into, and you can get through them quicker due to their flexible scheduling. Here are the pros and cons for this type of school:

Pros:

- Often less expensive than regionally accredited counterparts
- May require less liberal arts coursework
- May offer more practical, career-oriented majors
- May employ more relaxed admission standards

Cons:

- Credits not widely accepted if you later attend a regionally accredited college
- Coursework and degrees may not be accepted for professions that require licensing after attaining a degree, which might

affect those in licensed careers such as teaching, accounting, engineering, and healthcare

- Sometimes excluded from corporate tuition plans
- Sometimes provides self-study courses without instructor-led course sessions

Here's the thing, you need an education to move forward. Although I can spend all day telling you how important education is to your career and how to pace it so you don't look like a dude that isn't doing his real job, I still want to mention that you *must* be pursuing education if you want to be at the same caliber of the competition in today's bottled-up military. Simply put, work at a nationally accredited school can be done quicker and, in many cases, can be closely related to your Air Force Specialty Code (AFSC). I believe this is an important factor when it comes to master sergeant and senior master sergeant boards. Why wouldn't it be, right? I'm a firefighter and I completed my BS in fire science. Do you really think I wanted to do a fire science degree to set myself up for a job on the outside, let alone from a nationally accredited school? No way! It was simply a strategic approach to ensure the board could not look the other way when a candidate is going the extra mile to be more educated in his or her career field. They see it as a return on investment for the Air Force—and it is!

They (AF leadership) say a CCAF is not required for master sergeant, but the Air Force has changed. Job performance should *always* remain number one regarding any evaluation, but if you think you can sidestep education like the old-timers, you will be left behind. The fact is this, CCAF is a must in order to remain competitive in that segment, as is a bachelor's for senior master sergeant.

So when it comes to the military, a nationally accredited degree is just as good (and cheaper), *but* if you want to get a graduate degree that isn't directly related to your career field, you may want to go with the regional version. At the end of the day, it depends on what your long-term goals are and what you intend to do with the degree you've earned. If you absorb nothing else from this section, please use that *free* tuition assistance money!

What's Cool? AF COOL, That's What

Aside from the fact that you get a ridiculous amount of money to go to school, and the fact that you qualify for in-state tuition pretty much anywhere, regardless of whether or not you have residency status, you can also use some free money through AF COOL (Air Force Credentialing Opportunities On-Line). Back in the day, they advertised this as a vocational opportunity. Now, the AF COOL program has hundreds of offerings related to both your actual career field and general leadership. How cool is that? (Pun intended.)

All you have to do is log on to the portal and navigate to the virtual education center. You apply for a credential goal and work with the credentialing agency to figure out costs and prerequisites. You can even apply for more than one credential (with a maximum of $4,500). Let this free money work for you and pad that résumé!

About That GI Bill

This is important: If you have the old GI Bill, I strongly suggest you consider transferring to the new one. To me, the comparison isn't even close. Here are some stats:

Old Montgomery Bill

- Eligible for benefits for 10 years after separation or retirement
- No living expenses stipend
- No book stipend
- Monthly benefit capped at $1,648 per month for 36 months

New GI Bill (aka Post-9/11 GI Bill)

- Eligible for benefits for 15 years after separation or retirement
- BAH (basic allowance for housing) of an E-5 for living expenses
- Up to $1,000 for books

- 100 percent tuition costs for any public school
- Up to $22,805.34 per academic year

Five Tax Perks of the Air Force

At some point during your military career, you will take a hard look at your leave and earnings statement (LES) and try to play follow the money as you search exactly where it is all going. You may also see that although we use taxpayer money (a lot of taxpayer money) to operate, we also pay taxes just like everyone else. Well, don't worry, there are plenty of tax advantages built into your pay, and understanding them will help offset that "I don't get paid enough" feeling.

1. **Adjusted Gross Income (AGI)**: This is the best tax perk we have, in my opinion. You only pay federal tax on your base pay. This means that things like food pay (BAS), housing allowances, and cost of living adjustments aren't taxed! What a deal! So as far as the IRS knows, you are only making the equivalent salary of a part-timer at Taco Bell and therefore fall into a *very low* tax bracket.
2. **Combat Zone Tax Break**: As if there aren't enough reasons to raise your hand and beg to be deployed, not having to pay *any* tax makes deploying a must. When you are sent for an extended deployment, you won't pay taxes at all. When you file, just be sure you note that. That should save you a nice chunk right there.
3. **Itemize, Baby!** As a firefighter, I'm able to itemize basically anything. From food to equipment, the breaks are endless. As a military member, you can do the same thing. Take a look at your profession and see what additional things you can write off to make the tax break extra sweet. Items like personal protective equipment (PPE), contingency equipment, and haircuts are just a few you can easily write off.
4. **Charitable Donations**: Along with all the things we write off that you donate, you can also itemize your contributions to all the different organizations you contribute to. Examples include the Air Force Assistance Fund, the Combined Federal Campaign,

and professional organization membership dues. So give because you are a good person and give because you can also get some back! Two birds, one stone.

5. **The Small Things**: Like I said before, items like your BAS and housing allowance are not taxed. Neither are the hundreds of dollars you get each month for living overseas (which is highly recommended). For example, if you get $1,000 for housing, $300 for food, and $600 for living overseas each month, by the end of the year you've avoided over $22,000 in taxes! Remember, you are only taxed on your base pay.

Although we may not actually get paid at the same inflation rate as the employment cost index, we have perks galore just hanging out everywhere within our pay. Tax season is a time when we can smile or frown in the end. Hopefully, you are armed with all the ways you can help yourself take advantage of the military pay system. Good luck!

Random Awesome Benefits

I did some comprehensive benefit digging to make sure we are getting everything we can from *Uncle Sam*. The following awesome benefits came from over 200 hours of Internet research and discussions with many friends and peers to ensure no stone was left unturned. Now, I understand there is no way I have covered everything, so if you are already in the service and see that I'm missing something, help us all out and go to the *My Rich Uncle* website (simply type in this book title) and add it to the forum. We will all be grateful for your help! Without further ado, here is a collection of random benefits offered to us all.

The Library Quietly Kicks Ass

Yes, I know, its super cold in there, and if you sneeze more than once you feel like a jerk, but the library is exploding with benefits just waiting for you to take advantage of them. This melting pot of *free* stuff has something for us all. So let's look past the mundane furniture and terrible operating hours so we can all get informed on the following six ways libraries can help us maximize our enlistment:

1. It's freaking free: Although obvious, the library is one of the few places on earth where membership is free and all the benefits are included. Your ID card lands you a nicely laminated library keychain card that opens the door for more awesome things to come.

2. Digital subscriptions galore: That's right, there are literally hundreds (650) of the best magazine subscriptions available for *free*. Check out some of them at https://www. rbdigital.com/ aflis/service/ zinio/landing.

3. Ebook overload: Like to read? Obviously, you do. If you don't like to read, you will have a hard time getting ahead, because it is fundamental to growth. Now, we can't all be like Warren Buffet, who reads 250 pages a day, but we should be reading something, *anything*. The Air Force has basically dropped a miniature Kindle store for us, so you should check it out. Here's the link for that too: http:// af.lib.overdrive.com/59F5CCAD-B735-4F23-82CA-D52EDA529BDD/10/50/en/Default.htm.

4. Get your CLEP on: Don't want to go through a full course? I don't blame you. Time to bust out the CLEP/DANTE material and start accumulating those credits! The Air Force Online Library (just click Library on the AF Portal page) hooks you up with all the study material you need *free* of charge. Hey, maybe you are hardcore into education. Good! Because there is something called the Universal Class Program, which has over 540 online courses you can take.

5. The New Blockbuster Video: First, I wonder how many people don't even remember Blockbuster. Anyway, don't have Netflix? Don't need it. Each library has a jackpot of DVDs for *free*. From the big hits to your favorite TV shows, just go in, grab what you want, and enjoy. If you're lazy, that's cool too. Online programs like OverDrive have tons of music and videos to watch—all because you are military.

6. Free language programs—indeed: You can learn a language through various language-learning programs, all without spending a penny. Now this is muy bien! And yes, they have Rosetta Stone.

7. Working Wi-Fi: Today, this seems like a given. But if you have ever set foot on an Air Force base, you know Wi-Fi isn't everywhere. Sometimes the library is the only spot it's guaranteed to work. If you are super broke and can't afford Internet at home, just drive to the library parking lot and use some free Wi-Fi before heading home.

The list goes on and on. I'm telling you, this is a *huge* benefit that I don't think many people are capitalizing on. If you know of other sweet benefits that our library affords us, please leave it in the comments section so we can share the wealth.

The Home Base Program

Reduce PCS (permanent chance of station) costs and increase family stability!

Basically, if you are at a stateside (CONUS [Continental United States]) location and are selected to serve a short tour of 15 months or less, the Air Force will hook you up by returning you to the same CONUS location. With the exception of Alaska and Hawaii, you only have to make sure you have 7 months retainability (36 months for those two awesome locations). Moreover, you can't apply for a designated location move. (This program exists to aid active duty Airmen with foreign-born spouses who are unable to cope in the continental United States or overseas CONUS area during the airman's absence due to language barriers, lack of driver's license, etc.)

If you think this program is something you want to take advantage of, simply fill out the application on vMPF (virtual military personnel flight) no later than 150 days from the projected departure date. The online application should be read carefully, because it lays out *all* the rules and information you will need.

MRU Tip

Don't use the allowances to relocate dependents or store household goods (HHG). You can only use those funds to store goods if you are a single airman. If you are required to live off-base, you can ship HHG at the government's expense.

Remember, you can't use PCS (permanent chance of station) allowances, so if this causes a hardship, it isn't recommended to use the HB (home basing) program. More money questions can be answered in Attachment 5 of AFI 36-2110, Assignments.

If you are reading this and going through the process or if you already have approved orders, be sure the proper assignment remark is included in item 24 of the PCS order to ensure the FSO (flight safety officer) and TMO (traffic management officer) take actions that are consistent with the airman's HB agreement or advise the Military Personnel System (MPS) to cancel.

MRU Tip

You may have heard of the Follow-On Program (FO) where you can get preferred assignment consideration. People use this for a follow-on after a short tour. To make sure you have all your bases covered, be sure to look at section A5.6 in the Assignments AFI (Air Force instruction).

The Home Base Program should be used wisely but can have substantial family and financial benefits. If you have ever PCS'd, you know it can be super expensive to get all settled in again.

The Assignments Instruction Is Your Friend

Everyone cares about where they are going to be stationed. I mean, that could make or break you and your decision to stay in, right? A friend recently asked me about the Home Base Program and a light bulb went off in my head: Why not go through the assignments regulation (AFI 36-2110) and hook readers up with some random interesting notes? You may not need them now, but who knows?

- Deferment of PCS, TDY, and deployment for 12 months after you give birth.
- If you are a victim of stalking or any form of sexual misconduct, you can file for an expedited transfer with help from the Victim and Witness Assistance Program
- (2.6) When an airman is directed to make a PCS, the AF may not deny the airman any travel and transportation allowances associated with the PCS.
- The Voluntary Stabilized Base Assignment Program (VSBAP) (airmen only) provides a stabilized tour in exchange for volunteering for an assignment to a historically hard-to-fill location.

I Want to Be Stationed There!

Base of preference (BOP) is something many people want, but how do you make the right moves to ensure getting where you want to go? First, understand this is only for a CONUS (stateside) assignment. All good? Okay, here are some takeaways for your reading pleasure:

- This consists of two separate programs: the first-term airman (FTA) BOP program and the career airman BOP program. The FTA BOP program provides a reenlistment incentive under the Career Airmen Reenlistment Reservation System (CAREERS).
- Senior master sergeant and below? You meet that requirement.
- AFI 36-2110, attachment 2 is your go-to reference.
- You must have 24 months retainability. If you are a first-term airman (newbie), then you have to reenlist. Do both within 30 days of approval.
- Make sure you have an approved career job reservation (CJR)!
- You get one try, so don't mess it up!

Mil to Mil (rolling in the dough), you can do it to, but here are some specifics. The join spouse intent code is a major factor when considering a BOP request from an airman. If the intent code is A or B then both airmen must request the same location(s) in the same order (including in-place) or the request(s) will be disapproved. If approved, the BOP eligible airman will receive a BOP assignment whereas the spouse's assignment will be for joint spouse. When one airman of a military couple requests a BOP and the intent code is H, the request will be considered without regard to spousal preferences.

MRU Tip

Since BOP is determined by manning at the location requested, make sure your AFSC is low-manned where you want to go. vMPF (virtual military personnel flight) can help you out as well as the portal. If you put down a sweet spot like Florida, you won't be the only one!

I know, I know, I didn't mention everything. But, hey, hopefully this can be used as a nice guide if you are thinking about opting for a preferred base. Just remember, when you are overseas, you are in the game. When you are stateside, you are on the bench.

Other Awesome Benefits

- *Air Force Times* free subscription if you are active duty.
- The base-exchange (BX) is tax free. When you buy something expensive at the BX, be sure to use the warranty offering. If anything happens to your purchase, they will refund your money. I mean *anything* too.
- Air Force Clubs save money. Just be sure you save more than that damned monthly fee! Overseas, the E-Club usually offers free food for club members on Friday's. If you are overseas, it is definitely worth it. I honestly can't say the same for stateside.
- When you take a remote assignment, you apply for your follow-on through vMPF. You are first in line for whatever you choose (as long as there is a spot, of course). This benefit is a big deal! Who the hell wants to go to Clovis, New Mexico?
- Did you know as an active duty service member, your annual fees are waived for the American Express platinum card? Why

do you want this? I would say the 24-hour concierge service and entrance to luxury airline lounges would be a good start!

- The legal office will save you thousands by offering services you would have to pay for if you weren't maximizing your enlistment. Some sweet deals include:

  - Providing legal counsel
  - Preparing legal documents
  - Drafting powers of attorney
  - Reviewing contracts and leases
  - Estate planning advice
  - Notary services
  - Drafting wills
  - Tax advice

- Air Force Inns: After 4:00 p.m. anyone can reserve any available room. This includes all distinguished visitors (DV) and general suites. By regulation, the representative cannot deny you the room, regardless of rank.

- A financial advisor can cost you a pretty penny. Usually, it's a percentage of your investment, and at times it's a flat fee, often over $1,500. We have this service for *free*! Like I've said before, head down to Airman and Family Readiness Center and get sound advice from a certified, licensed financial advisor.

- If you are a member of the armed forces on active duty and you move because of a permanent change of station, you are entitled to a deduction for reasonable nonreimbursed moving expenses related to travel and the cost of moving household goods and personal effects. Be sure to check out the details at the Armed Forces Tax (http://www.irs.gov/pub/irs-pdf/p3.pdf).

Want *free* money? Enter a scholarship contest with an organization on base! Very few people enter and it's *free* cash if you win! How easy is that? As much as $250 for 30 minutes of your time is a great value.

You Can Bet Your SGL(ife) on It

I always used to say, "If I die, who cares who gets money? I'm dead!" Well, that's not the right way to think. Aside from the fact that life costs, you know, money is the fact that we can't be so selfish to not ensure we provide for those we love even after we pass away.

Here's the thing, the Service Group Life Insurance (SGLI) may not be the best program but it's easily accessible. I think the reason everyone goes down that road is because it is a readily available method to a whopping $400K. Don't believe me? Let's take a look at the numbers.

SGLI is pretty sweet because it's automatic. If you are active duty, you're in. Payouts come in $50,000 increments all the way up to a maximum $400K. I think the big-time benefit of this is that you get 120 days of coverage for *free* after separation. Hopefully you aren't disabled, but if you are, you can extend that *free* coverage up to two years.

As of 2014, SGLI cost $29 a month. Not bad, right? SGLI currently costs 7 cents per $1,000 of coverage. The rate rises though, and the future is unpredictable. This is only while you are active duty, of course. When you are all done with this rodeo, you can opt for VGLI (Veteran Group Life Insurance). But VGLI rates are almost double what you pay while active duty. Yikes!

One cool thing about VGLI is that if you enroll within 240 days of your "I am finally out!" date, you don't have to talk about all those health issues. But VGLI rates are hardcore. For example, let's say I was super young when I enlisted and I served 20 years. I would be 38 years old, and the current rate for those guys is $52! Imagine if you came in late! If you retire between 40 and 44 years of age, you pay $88. No thanks!

There is a better deal (in my opinion anyway). Give it up for **USAA**! Yep, the bank we all love also provides life insurance and is actually a better deal in the long run. Here's why. USAA locked me in at $32 for the next 30 years. Why is this important? Well, if you are anything like me, your body gets worse as time goes on. With poorer overall health come higher premiums for life insurance. Having it locked in at a low rate is a tremendous benefit! Who's to say in the next 30 years the SGLI premiums won't rise well above that $3 difference?

MRU Tip
You can convert your SGLI to one of many approved commercial life insurance companies that will be much less than that horrible VGLI premium. Here's a link to a list of participating companies: http://www.benefits.va.gov/ INSURANCE/converting.asp

Take Leave the Right Way

Name another job where you are simply an employee to a larger corporation and yet you get 30 vacation days a year? And it's paid vacation too! It would be difficult to find this type of deal in the civilian world. In the military, not only do we get those 30 days, calculated at 2½ days per month, but we can also take different types of leave. Our rich uncle hooked us up here as well, and here are a few things I was able to pull from AFI 32-3003 *Air Force Leave Policy*:

- All members should have the opportunity to take at least one leave period of 14 consecutive days or more every fiscal year (FY) and are encouraged to use the 30 days accrued each FY.

- You are qualified for payment of accrued leave upon re-enlistment, retirement, separation under honorable conditions, or death. It limits payment of accrued leave to 60 days in a military career.

- Members separating under Palace Chase/Palace Front may carry any unused leave over as long as there is no break in service.

- A member is on leave status after working at least 50 percent of the duty day, and the following day is the first day of chargeable leave.

- You may be able to take up to 30 days of convalescent leave to recuperate from a medical procedure. If you were treated at a

Military Treatment Facility (MTF), they can grant up to 90 days. For maternity leave, you get 84 days. All nonchargeable.

- Permissive TDY (PTDY) is nonchargeable leave and your squadron commander can authorize 10 days for all sorts of things. This is the best part of the leave instruction and can be leveraged to attend conferences, seminars, secure off-base housing, job searches, attend meetings with direct correlation to your job, attend professional conventions, take license/certification tests, lead religious programs, retreats, adoptions, parental leave for guys, and more. Everyone should take some time to study Table 4.5.

MRU TIP

Ever notice the reenlistment option when you are selecting the leave type on LEAVEWEB? When you reenlist, consider requesting a special leave pass from your commander. This can either be a three- or four-day pass. There's a catch, though: you may have to use it in conjunction with a weekend. But, hey, at least it's some free leave!

Don't Worry, the VA Has Your Back

The first of many times spraining my ankle pretending my goofy white ass could play basketball, a friend mentioned that I should ensure this was noted in my medical records. I think most of us have heard this one already, right? Those crazy medical records that for whatever reason end up disappearing if you aren't carefully watching over them and making copies at certain intervals. It turns out, those records are really important. When my friend reminded me of this, she was referring to injuries you can claim when you receive your discharge from the military. It wasn't until I bothered to search "Veterans Affairs Benefits" online that I realized how impactful Veterans Affairs (VA) is on all our lives. There is so much to maximize!

Any time you have an issue, injury, or illness, you should go to your primary care provider and make sure it gets documented. In my time thus far, some of the most common things I have seen that I know have a high probability for post-retirement compensation include:

- Back injuries
- Hazardous chemical exposure
- On-duty injuries
- Deployment issues
- Asbestos

Veteran benefits are earned through honorable service. Knowing what VA benefits are available will assist you in taking advantage of the many programs once you are out of this awesome Air Force. Don't worry, my good friend and VA specialist Kristal will run down a few ways you can prepare yourself:

- Create an ebenefits account with your CAC (your ID) before you turn it in: https://www.ebenefits.va.gov/ebenefits/ home page. Do not create your account using your .mil email account.
- Request a full copy of your medical records, and make a copy of that copy for yourself. Make sure you have everything documented prior to getting out of the service. If you have knee pain and never went to the doctors about it, go to a doctor before getting out. It makes VA claims very difficult if you have no medical documentation of the injury during your service.
- Make sure your military records are complete, and make a copy of them. For example, if you deployed to Afghanistan and your records are missing your campaign medal, fix it before you get out. (After Kristal wrote this, I immediately ran a quick check and noticed two issues on my record!)
- Triple check your DD-214 draft with MPF before you approve the draft.
- If you have at least four years of retainability, sign your GI Bill over to your dependents, even if they will not use it. It's good to have options.
- Get that CCAF before you get out! You cannot complete it after your date of separation.

- If you're six months from separation, you can apply for vocational rehab through Ebenefits.va.gov. They can assist you in making a plan for life after the service.
- Prior to leaving the service apply for one of the following to get your VA disability claim started:
- Benefits Delivery at Discharge (BBD)
- Quick Start
- Overseas Intake Sites
- Go to Transition Assistance Program (TAPs). Take notes, ask questions, and create a résumé!

Now, let's talk a little about disability benefits. If you wait to file VA disability until after you have received your DD-214, you should file your VA disability claim before the one-year mark of your date of separation. There are many free organizations to assist you in filing your VA claim.

MRU Tip

If you file your VA disability claim 364 days after separation, and it takes the VA a year to complete your claim and give you a rating, the VA will not only provide back pay to the date you filed but also back pay to the date you separated from the service.

For example, your date of separation is January 1, 2017, and you file your VA disability claim on December 31, 2017. Your rating is completed on December 31, 2018, and you are rated 60 percent. The VA will back pay you to January 1, 2017. A veteran alone, without children, would receive $1,062.27 a month for a 60 percent rating, so you would receive about 24 months of back pay, a total of $25,494.48. If you waited to file your claim until January 2, 2017, then you would only receive about 12 months of back pay. You can check the most current compensation table at http://www.benefits.va.gov/compensation/resources_comp01.asp.

Note: If you received a severance payment when you left the service, you cannot collect VA disability until it is repaid.

Medically Tri-to-Care

"Here, take this Motrin and it should be better soon."
— The Military Doctor Perception

So many people complain about the military medical system. Honestly, I don't get it. Sure, it isn't perfect, but it's superior to what you would get these days in the civilian world. What other job can you freely go to the clinic for *anything* at any time? In my opinion, the issue, as in the case with the civilian side, is that doctors are treating symptoms and not root causes.

One way to maximize your medical benefits is to go through the wickets and get a referral to a specialist for your issue. Tricare will cover it, and having a specialist for free is quite a perk!

Dental Tips from a Dude with Lots of Cavities

The military dental system is pretty good. Typically you hear grumbles and myths about the level of effectiveness in the military health care system, but in the case of dental care, it is indeed a myth. In fact, military dentists are well trained, usually in their prime, and consistent in both performance and communication with patients.

The trick to getting the most out of your dental benefit is to talk to your hygienist-technician. Usually only a few years into the military, they will hook you up with the perks. For example, you can get a free cleaning twice a year. That may not seem like much, but go price professional cleanings on the outside. Furthermore, if you really don't like your teeth and they're affecting your stress levels and work performance (or at least you feel they are), then you can get the military to pay for some big-time transformational, cosmetic procedures! Lastly, make your appointment first thing in the morning. You don't have to wake up as early, because the first appointment is at 0730. This buys you a little snooze time, and there is very little waiting time once you arrive at the dentist's office.

Making sure you trust your doc is important no matter what, and it's no exception here. There is usually an abundance of teeth pullers, so you can easily request a different one if you are not satisfied with your care. Just let your technician know. I don't see this happen often, though, because these guys know what they are doing.

Don't believe the myths about military dental care.

MRU Tip

Ask about an additional cleaning after six months, and if they deny you, simply ask to reference the regulation. I successfully get the extra cleaning four out of six times.

Chapter 7

See the World on Uncle Sam's Dime

Temporary Duty: Permanent Memories

Going on a temporary duty assignment (TDY) is, for me, the most exciting part of being in the Air Force. There is something about being on the road in a new territory that really gets me fired up. I have been very fortunate during my career to be selected for so many sweet TDYs, and I know for a fact that it goes back to setting yourself up within the organization. Credibility goes a long way, and the more you build it, the higher your chance of being asked to go somewhere on behalf of the organization.

Over the last 12 years, I have enjoyed TDYs to Scotland, Spain, the Philippines, Holland, Romania, Germany, and more. There were many amazing things about the trips, but in general, there are five things they each have in common that made them great:

1. **Per Diem:** This is of course number one because who doesn't love money? The military will send you to a really sweet place, put you up in a nice, clean hotel, and then, when you come back, you get paid for doing it! If this isn't the best incentive to get yourself a TDY, I don't know what is! Even if you get the minimum ($3.50 a day), over time it racks up. Some places, Holland, for example, lands you $188 a day in per diem. Wow! The idea behind this is to offset the costs associated with this official business trip. I would say the best example of per diem in my experience was when I went to the Philippines for the

Balikitan exercise and had the time of my life, only to come back and bank over $3,000 in per diem. Now that is awesome.

2. **Meet New People**: You would be surprised how many great people you meet when you're on the road. Many of the countries in this vast world of ours are laid out on the premise of people first. This leads to meeting some of the nicest, most caring individuals in countries you never thought you would ever visit. Along with the natives of the countries, the people you join on TDYs usually end up becoming your friends for a very long time. This is due to the fact you are sharing these unique experiences that only those who were there can relate to. Be sure to make friends immediately when given a TDY opportunity.

3. **Hotels**: Seriously, the government hooks you up on hotels when you are out of the country. Because force protection is always an issue, the military figures they should put you in a prominent hotel because it's taxpayer money and our people need to be safe (and spoiled). It is very rare that you are put in anything less than a four-star hotel. Everything from fire detection to the neighborhood is a factor, so you are usually setting your GPS to a place where the rooms look like something out of an Ikea catalog. Be sure to get breakfast included in the price of the room. You can even do this after you arrive, if the government hasn't already. When you pay with your Government Travel Card, it reads as lodging, but you also get free breakfasts.

4. **Stories**: The number of stories that build up as a result of TDYs are boundless. If you were to ask someone in the military to tell a story about something that happened while in the service, it typically starts with, "Okay, so I was TDY to . . . " This is due to the fact that going TDY is a setup for a great time!

5. **Recharging**: I can't tell you how good it feels to do something enjoyable and then return home ready to dominate. Maybe it's all the beer and laughter, or maybe it's just daydreaming out the car window. Whatever it is, it seems like you are as refreshed as can be after a TDY. I usually come back to work armed with a nice set of goals to knock out while I'm fully charged. My advice to

make the most of this is to write a short list of things you want to accomplish as soon as you return, and then make sure you actually do it. Now go have some fun!

GTC Tips While TDY

Did you hear about the person who got hemmed up due to Government Travel Card (GTC) misuse? It happens, and it would suck if you got caught in that web. When you are TDY and you have to use your GTC, you want to be sure you are using it for the right things. Here are three tips that may help you out:

1. **Use it for everything**: Why? Because it is mandatory, that's why.

2. **Don't think it builds credit**: The GTC isn't like your little $400-limit credit card your credit union issued you. It doesn't help you build credit. With that said, keep the balances super low! To contrast, if you don't pay your bill within 210 days, that will affect your credit score.

3. **Ensure your GTC is Defense Travel System (DTS) ready**: Too often I see people having mad issues when trying to either make a purchase or file a voucher because their GTC wasn't linked up properly. Call your DTS people to make that happen pronto. While you're at it, call Citibank and make sure they know you are traveling and not to block your usage (this actually happens).

TDYs are amazing experiences and possibly the best part of being in the Air Force. Just be sure you know what you are doing with Uncle Sam's credit card so you don't inadvertently screw yourself.

MRU Tip:
When booking a room on your GTC, bed-and-breakfasts are the way to go. You typically receive better service than a hotel, and breakfast is included without taking anything away from your per diem. This saves $10 to $15 a day, easy. Of course, this is if you have the option to choose your hotel.

Positioning Yourself

"If your plan isn't working, change the plan, not the goal."
— Darren Hardy

Do you think it's an accident that one guy always gets the sweet TDYs? You think it's the luck of the Irish that Airman Smith landed another awesome deployment? It would be semidelusional to think that opportunities are given by random chance in your organization. Sure, sometimes manning and mission needs force someone out the door at times, but more often than not, leadership is selective about who they send out, and it is on you to know how to position yourself within the organization to reap those sweet benefits. A few examples during my time come to mind that are worth sharing.

In 2005 we had a taser drop for two weeks in Scotland. I was stationed at Ramstein AB, Germany, at the time, and this sounded like a nice opportunity to see the land of Loch Ness! Leadership sent it out to the lead supervisors on each shift to collect names. They needed someone with a P-19 (a certain type of firetruck) license, a passport, and someone who had completed their upgrade training. Since there were only a few of us that met those conditions, I was already in the running. Because I had trained most guys on the P-19 at the time, I was lucky enough to get selected. We ended up working for four days before driving all over Scotland, staying at hostels, and playing Capture the Castle at the castle from Braveheart! This would have never happened if I hadn't met those simple requirements.

In 2006, the Bomberos of Moron AB, Spain, needed some firefighters to fill in for them while they attended training. The tanker was for a couple months, and of course, I wanted in on that action! The only reason I got to go was because I had completed all my upgrade training and happened to have a license on the particular truck they had. How simple is that? In fact, we even got to be a part of a space shuttle mission! The trip to Spain was one of the most memorable of my life, and it happened because I made sure I met all requirements, all the time, if anything ever came up. I'm not special. You can do this too. I assure you it will pay off.

Positioning yourself in the organization is all about being proactive. Are you the one who trains others? Are you ahead on all of your training? Do you arrive first and leave last? These things leave lasting impressions on your supervisors and leaders. Because I have followed this set of rules throughout my career, I have been able to see so many places, and all the while getting paid! Take a minute and think of all the ways you can ensure you are positioned well within your organization. If not, what do you need to do to become more visible? It could be that you are not well suited in your current position and need a change or that your supervisor is not vocal about your impact to the mission. These things can change, and before you know it, you will be at the front of the line when a sweet TDY comes up.

A Matter of Perspective

Have you ever met someone and thought they were stupid only to find out they are brilliant? What about the opposite? That guy we met at the newcomers brief sure is intelligent. Fast-forward a few weeks and we find out he is subpar at pretty much everything. This happens throughout our lives. First impressions may or may not be consistent with the long-term perspective of an individual. In the Air Force, it appears most things are solely dependent on perspective. That guy just gave a really great brief. He must be an all-star!

MRU Tip
Use this to your advantage by "wowing" the audience with an idea, service or product.

The story goes like this. I knew, as we all know, I had to check certain boxes in order to remain competitive in this hunger-games environment, so I knew I needed to land an executive position in one of the installation's private organizations. Since I have a decent history in this type of function, I aimed high (no AF pun intended) for a spot on the Wing Top III. If you aren't familiar, this is the organization for SNCOs and every base has one. Top III is actually great, and the networking alone is worth the free admission price.

Using the law of recency, I decided to do something big right before the election. Their website was outdated and needed some love, so I charted a plan to improve it and have the new site launch just prior to the elections. I gave the brief and the team loved it. Now, I would have done this anyway, because I'm always looking for ways to improve things, but how convenient was it that it happened at the right time.

As a new SNCO, the majority of voters may not have known anything about me, but when it came time to vote, my name had become synonymous with something positive. Is this why I ended up winning that election? I don't know, but I'm certain it didn't hurt! You see, there is a psychological thing that happens when you present yourself a certain way, and the law of recency can help.

My advice is to purposely find something that needs improving, make it awesome, and then sell it at the right time. The fact of the matter is this, being an executive has promotion implications attached to it, and if you can find ways to ensure you're in the running, make it happen.

Chapter 8

Leadership in a Follower's World

Define Who You Are

> *"A leader is one who knows the way,*
> *goes the way, and shows the way."*
> — John C. Maxwell

Leadership is one of those buzzwords we love to throw around as if everyone *needs* to be a leader. It makes you feel like you're selling everyone short if they're not labeled as a leader. I remember wondering exactly what the hell a leader is and whether or not I could ever be one. Leadership was elusive and daunting all at the same time. A far cry from my position at the time as a "you don't know anything" airman, but I did a little digging and realized that leadership has different definitions, depending on whom you talk to. Many agree it is different from being a manager, and it is. You know that NCOIC (non-commissioned officer in charge) who is simply making sure things get done so the master sergeant doesn't light him up? Well, he is managing, not leading.

After looking up my now favorite leadership author, John C. Maxwell, I see there are two fundamental principles that define a leader inside or outside of the military. They are broad but true:

1. A leader makes individuals *want* to do whatever it is you need them to do.

2. Leadership is all about influence. Nothing more, nothing less.

I know you're thinking this is too general and leadership is much more than these two principles. You're right, but as you will find out throughout this chapter, everything falls under these two principles in one way or another. That staff sergeant who is simply making sure things get done is not leading. What happens if he turns his back? Will the work still get done? What if he takes leave for a week? That staff sergeant is a leader if his people truly want to get the work done. That's the key, ladies and gentlemen. They *want* to do it.

One of the most discerning things I ever heard that sticks with me anytime I'm in a position to lead was on a Brian Buffini podcast. He was interviewing the great football coach Lou Holtz. The coach said that when you become a leader in any situation, human beings all have the same three questions:

1. Can I trust you?

2. Are you good at what you do?

3. Do you care about me?

Try to really digest those. If you keep them in mind and tailor your words and actions to the folks in your unit, I don't see how you could not be successful, at least on the human level.

Now that we have introduced the basic training of leadership, it is a good idea to get momentum (my favorite word) and begin your path to becoming a true enlisted leader. Taking a page from NCOA (Non-Commissioned Officer Academy), I recommend you create a personal leadership development plan. This really sets the stage for your own success (goals are our destinations in life), and it also creates the necessary momentum to initiate a following of dedicated airmen who will follow in your footsteps. Below is the plan I created during my time in NCOA.

Personal Leadership Development Plan
for TSGT Andrew Kehl
Kisling Noncommissioned Officer Academy

November 29, 2014

Instructor: TSGT Brian Cravo

Part I: Personal Values

My top five values are:

1. **Gratitude**: My top value is to be gracious for the abundance in my life. The environment we are born into is simply the luck of the draw, and if we are lucky enough to be born in a place that provides opportunity, we need to ensure we are grateful every day. I understand the magnitude of poverty in the world and wake up every day saying "thank you" for what I have been given. Gratitude will always come first.

2. **Family**: Being a leader means having your head on straight. To be effective personally or professionally, we must have a solid foundation. This comes from my family, and without it, I could not build. The foundation your family provides allows you to thrive in this world, and without them, success would be a distant dream.

3. **Inspiration**: Valuing inspiration comes from constantly sharpening your leadership saw. Reading is an essential habit that inspires me. I feed my mental hunger and do my best to roll that into quality relationships, effective management, and humble leadership. Everyone wants to be inspired, and leadership effectiveness, in my opinion, cannot be accomplished without it.

4. **Adventure**: Being adventurous means trying new things, meeting new people, and getting into the habit of saying yes. I value meeting new people and trying new things. This allows me to build my global network of friends and colleagues, further enhancing my leadership potential. Moreover, I believe life itself is an adventure. Like Gandhi said, "Live like you will die tomorrow, learn like you will live forever."

5. **Confidence**: In order to be a respectable leader, you need to be confident. Nobody likes a pessimist or a person with low self-esteem. Being confident means you believe in yourself and what you can do in this world. It means making decisions based on morals and ethics and not allowing others to negatively affect you. I value my confidence and work on it every day.

Part II: Leadership Vision Statement

As a leader, I want to reach my definition of success while being both humble and influential. I would like to be the type of leader people feel comfortable approaching and having a desire to work for, regardless of whether or not I'm present. This would be my definition of leader influence.

It is vitally important to me that my subordinates are inspired based on my example. I understand that leading by example is the most difficult aspect of leadership and I welcome the challenge.

With a wonderful family supporting me, I believe my proverbial "leadership lid" is endless. Through gained knowledge, I'm confident in my decision-making abilities and will do my best to demonstrate that every day of the week. These and my other top values are what I use to propel me on my journey and solidify the morals and ethics I incorporate in those decisions.

In the future I hope that my leadership abilities are not bound to the rank I wear on my sleeve, but instead on my influential characteristics. My peers see reality in the perceptions we set every day, so it is crucial I influence them to desire the very best for all those around them. In my career field, we need one another, and without positive team dynamics, we will fail at our job. Each person has an essential role and we must remember to complete rather than compete with one another.

Finally, as a leader, I want to maximize referent, informational, and expert leadership powers to have the majority of my peers operating on the involvement tier of the contemporary motivation model. If this happens, I know everyone will be internally motivated, and it will not matter what is asked of them, because they will gain satisfaction, self-worth, and gratification regardless. This will be the culminating point where I feel I will reach my definition of success.

Part III: Strength and Improvement Areas

Throughout this life I identified and related to many of the self-assessments and lesson principles we covered in class. After taking some time to think, I have come up with three strengths and three weaknesses I will identify and elaborate on for my development action plan. My strengths include followership, personal power, and inspirational motivation. My weaknesses include (but are definitely not limited to) communicating, developing airmen, and using the three Ps when making decisions.

Regarding my strengths, I believe I do a decent job demonstrating followership because I show initiative and competence in my workplace. Furthermore, I always provide feedback and give advice to my supervisors.

Personal power was added to the brief list of strengths because I fit into the qualities of referent, information, and expert powers.

Last, I finished the list with inspirational motivation because, as an integral component of who I am, it serves as the one that, if embodied, is always optimistic and enthusiastic about the future.

In my opinion, our strengths need to shine in order to gain a positive perception and help the organization. I may only be good at a few things, but I will try to excel in those things until I have mastered them. My two best strengths are leading and speaking. I use these to my advantage anytime I can. These strengths and others have defined my essence. My essence, or at least what I hope my essence is to some, is inspiring. I say this not because I'm special but because I see the special in others and try to lead by example. It is our duty as NCOs to help the younger generation grow, and we must be able to inspire them in order to do so.

Regarding my weaknesses, I feel I could communicate better by providing characteristics such as listening, justifying, and feedback.

Developing airmen was added to this portion of the list because I feel I could pay closer attention to my subordinates' traits, such as personality, focus, and attitude.

Last, the three Ps round out my weakness list because their focus (principle, purpose, people) should be used for every decision, which I think I fall short at occasionally.

Part IV: Development Action Plan

Action Plan:

A good action plan not only places aspirations on paper but also shows you how to achieve the desired results. This is what I aim to accomplish as I move forward in creating a SMART (specific, measurable, acceptable, realistic, timeframe) action plan.

People say, "We need to work on our weaknesses first." But I do not believe this to be true. I feel we should place the majority of effort in our strengths so we can truly shine. With that said, immediate attention will be on my inspirational motivation. With the proper attitude, anything can be accomplished, and I will remember this as I focus attention on waking up every day, simply thankful to be alive. I will take five minutes at the end of each day to reflect and make sure I'm meeting my expectations to remain positive throughout the day. Second, I will improve on my personal power by sitting down with each of my airmen to measure their commitment. From there I will take time at the end of each week to make sure I'm accurately obtaining the right data and information from my subordinates while remaining influential by leveraging my expert power. To achieve this, I will need to make sure I read at least one organizational policy, guide, or regulation per day. While focusing on my strengths, I will ensure I provide weekly feedback to my supervisors and continue to be the first to raise my hand when a challenge presents itself.

A weakness is like dirty laundry; you know you have plenty, but you don't feel like doing much about it. Although there is some truth to that odd analogy, it is crucial we take the first step and identify what we are weak at. This will allow us to eventually get to where we write an action plan and begin the improvement process. Communicating is something I do very well (only sometimes in the wrong context). To be effective, I will make a specific task for myself to thoroughly explain directions when delegating. Additionally, before accepting a task, I will ensure only active listening is happening. Often I find myself passively listening when I become uninterested. To measure my communicating endeavor, I will ask for feedback to ensure everything is clear. Similarly, I will harness this positive energy as I work on better developing my airmen. This can improve by getting to know all of the airmen in my workplace on a deeper and more personal level. Once my action plan begins, I will create a document that contains key information about each person. Examples of key information include age, birthday, spouse, kids, hobbies, etc. I believe once I have a good grasp on who a person is, I can begin building on the institutional competencies of the "Develops Self" foundation.

Over the next three to five years, I will implement the above action plan. Throughout the entire process I will reiterate whether or not it is SMART and, when available, seek specific training for development. If I do so, success will be inevitable. (See, I'm already improving my inspirational motivation!)

A few leadership quotes that motivate me to being the best version of myself and I hope will bring out the best in you as well:

> *"A good leader is a person that takes a little more of his share of the blame and a little less than his share of the credit."*
> — John Maxwell

> *"Perfection is not attainable, but if we chase perfection we can catch excellence."*
> — Vince Lombardi

> *"To handle yourself, use your head; to handle others, use your heart."*
> — Eleanor Roosevelt

> *"When everything seems to be going against you, remember that the airplane takes off against the wind, not with it."*
> — Henry Ford

> *"The quality of a leader is reflected in the standards they set for themselves."*
> — Ray Kroc

How Valuable Are You?

Average is awesome. Everyone loves average. Average will get you by. Are you average? The thing is, the average person in the military will come to work, not get in trouble, follow all the rules, and then go home for a little rinse-and-repeat action. Seth Godin, in *Linchpin: Are You Indispensable?*, wrote that average comes from two places:

1. You have been brainwashed by school and by the system to believe that your job is to do your job and follow instructions. It isn't.

2. Everyone has a little voice inside their head that's angry and afraid. That voice is resistance, and it wants you to be average (and safe).

Does this sound familiar? It did to me for a long time, and until you commit to not being average, you will continue in the same cycle, letting hundreds of opportunities pass you by. You can get by with this because the Air Force still provides attendance-based compensation. But is this how you want to get through? Isn't this how all those crusty old SNCOs got through, simply by showing up for long enough?

Godin was spot-on when he described how you get what you get. He noted, "If you want a job where it's okay to follow the rules, don't be surprised if you get a job where following the rules is all you do." I love it. If you want the type of job where your subordinates do exactly what you tell them to do, why on earth would you be surprised if your boss does the exact same thing to you? Isn't that what you wanted?

On the contrary, if you want to do more than simply follow instructions, you will find you will be asked to do things that aren't a part of the traditional school curriculum. If you want a job where you use your brain to make things happen and take risks, don't be surprised if you are quickly promoted. It's that simple.

This has a trickle-down effect. Creativity needs to flow in order for your organization to be successful. Do you think your workplace would be more successful if everyone was more obedient? I doubt it. Make the switch now. Free your people up and create more value by letting them be creative, artistic, passionate, and connected.

There is an interesting value in the power of saying no. How often do you use it? There are a few people who can get to yes regardless of the request. Those people just make shit happen. Boom. Done. Who doesn't want that? Then there are those linchpins that use the power of no. They say no because they have goals, they have a vision. It is about having the courage to be disappointing in the short term in order to provide true value later. The point is, you can add more value to yourself by remaining focused and understanding that, with good intent, saying no is also a priceless trait.

Being able to say no implies you are in a position to say no. For example, if you have value to the community, maybe you will be asked to lead this or that or to take a certain position or chair a certain event. Being able to say no has prevented me from getting myself into too much and spreading myself too thin. At work, if you are not in the right position due to rank, you can achieve the same by masking the unimportant with high-value tasks and projects. Telling your boss you will get to something but there are higher priorities takes courage, I know. But the ability to do this cannot be overstated. Try it.

Creating value means making the most of any situation. The optimist, as I stated before, will rise above the rest because they will add value despite perceived dissatisfaction. The story of Bill and Nancy goes like this. Bill hates his job. He sees customers all day but doesn't provide much value to them. He won't even look them in the eye. Bill maximizes his breaks and is always complaining. Bill feels like he isn't being paid enough and sits in a lull he refuses to get out of. Nancy, though, does the same thing Bill does, but she does it with a smile. She sees this job as a platform to something bigger. Nancy makes a little difference and adds a little value to her customers every day. Who do you think will see the raise? Who will move forward? I'm reminded of the many times I heard people say, "I will do this or that at my next job" or "I will take that class once I PCS [permanent chance of station] and am settled." No, you won't. You have the power to create value today.

Eight Leadership Lessons I Have Learned

In 2015 I had an opportunity to give a presentation on leadership to members of RE/MAX in sunny Arizona. I felt like I was on a TED Talk or something and surprised by the enthusiasm of the professionals and how well they received my briefing. Subsequently, my friends thought it would be cool to have it in the book. I hope it is of some value to you as we all work every day to become more effective leaders.

Lesson #1: Habits are like a comfortable bed—easy to get into, hard to get out of.

- Successful people have proactive habits. Read Stephen Covey's *The Seven Habits of Highly Effective People: Restoring the Character Ethic* (1989).
- According to Psychology Today, habits take an average of 62 days to form.
- Aristotle was correct, you are what you repeatedly do.
- Self-awareness test: Choose a habit you desire and see if you can do it for 62 days. It should become second nature for you. What will you choose?

Lesson #2: Not everyone gets a trophy.

- Bottom line up-front: If a leader ignores the top performers, they lose their winning edge. If a leader rewards the weak performers, they never develop a winning edge.
- Honest feedback is critical. Feedback needs to come from both superiors and peers. The importance of peer feedback cannot be overstated.
- We never get what we deserve; we get what we earn.

Lesson #3: If you want to fly with eagles, don't hang around with turkeys.

- We are a product of our environment and those with whom we associate with shape our future, good or bad.
- Are the people around you making you better? Are they challenging you? If not, lose them or lose yourself.

Lesson #4: They don't care how much you know; they want to know how much you care.

- Whatever your profession, do they know you genuinely care? You can be the smartest person in the place, but it's difficult to lead those who won't follow.

Strength and Improvement Areas

Strengths	Improvement Areas
Followership	Communicating
Personal power	Developing airmen
Inspirational motivation	The three Ps

- What are we doing for each other? Remember, we need to complete, not compete.
- I had to learn the hard way. I made it a point to know as much as possible about my job, but it wasn't until I put real feelings toward my peers and subordinates that I really began to grow.

Lesson #5: You don't know what you can get away with until you try.
- Asking for forgiveness rather than permission has its place in life.
- It's not about abusing situations but about knowing when to push the boundaries.
- Think BIG!

Lesson #6: A bad process will beat a great person every time.
- Are you familiar with lean thinking? It's critical we focus our attention on the elimination of non-value-added steps in our processes.
- What process do you have when you're working with a client through a sale? Is it all value-added from the customer's perspective?
- Eight wastes: transportation, excess inventory, motion, waiting, overproduction, overprocessing, defects, and underutilization of human potential.

Lesson #7: If you swim with the stream, you're most likely a dead fish.
- What new, innovative opportunities exist in your profession?
- The status quo is the quiet way people resist looking at things in a way that disrupts the flow of the way things are done.
- "When everyone thinks alike, then no one is thinking."—Benjamin Franklin

Lesson #8: Focus on impact.
- Put your emphasis on the four quadrants of time and their impact on your productivity.
- Q2 baby! (The quadrant that matters.)
- Signs and symptoms of not adhering to Lesson #8: You work hard all day only to go home feeling like you accomplished nothing.
- Italian economist Vilfredo Pareto (1848–1923) gave us the following 80/20 rules. They apply everywhere!
- 20 percent of the work will result in 80 percent of the output.
- 20 percent of employees are responsible for 80 percent of the output.
- Leverage your strengths and minimize your effort on weaknesses.

I did not create these leadership lessons, but I accumulated them over the last 13 years from outstanding people with real experiences. These lessons have been distilled to what I perceive as lessons that apply directly to everyone in the armed forces. Keep them in that toolbox of yours and I believe they will be of great use for you. Remember that leadership is all about influence and caring. This can be extremely difficult, so begin running through these now and reap those leadership dividends.

Teamwork Makes the Dream Work

"None of us are as smart as all of us."
— Ken Blanchard

In the Air Force, and presumably the rest of the military, it is more and more a corporate world, full of head bashing to get ahead. Is that the new way to get promoted? Hell, yeah! I'm in and screw everyone else! We must get better at building teams and celebrating wins together. When you go to your fellow airman and ask him or her how you can add value to their day, you have just planted a seed for organizational growth that cannot be underestimated.

In leadership, it's the team that will propel your individual efforts to the next level. One cannot simply go off alone into the wilderness and have an expectation to climb the ladder to the top of the enlisted ranks. Sure, you can delegate everything once you get enough rank on your sleeve to do so. But I believe it's better to leverage a different type of power that we aren't capitalizing on as much as we should. You see, your authority as an NCO, for instance, comes from two places: legal authority and earned authority. The former is what I see being overused. NCOs have the right to use the Uniform Code of Military Justice and enforce standards and obedience. This will keep the ship afloat, because standards and obedience are the concrete on which we build our pillars. With that said, earned power will get you and your team to the next level. This is the type of authority that is given to a leader by her or his peers and subordinates. When you know you want to follow someone because they lead by example and have your interests in mind, you give them this type of authority. If you ever want to know who has it in your life, ask yourself, "Who do I truly respect?"

Professor Richard Florida of the University of Toronto polled thousands of professionals to weigh the factors that motivated them to do their best work. The top five, in order, are:

1. Challenge and responsibility
2. Flexibility
3. A stable work environment
4. Money

5. Professional development

Take this list and ask yourself if you are being a part of the team or not. Only a team can make big moves to propel an organization forward.

MRU Tip
Surround yourself with people who talk about visions and ideas, not other people.

Keeping It Real on Equatability in the AF

Part of the teamwork discussion has to include my keeping it real. We, as active duty members, are faced with some challenges we need to recognize and vocalize in order for some things to change. There are so many amazing people in the military, but we still find ways as a corporation to make things quite unfair.

Let's say you have eight people of the same rank in your work center. Is the workload equitable? Are all eight equally contributing to the organization? If not, why are they paid the same as the next guy (or more if they have been around longer)? Does seniority deserve higher pay or does work performance? Is attendance-based compensation acceptable? Of course, these are rhetorical questions. So I posted them on social media where my AF friends could provide some feedback. Here are a few of their answers, some serious, some hilarious:

In the civilian world, you can have people with the same title [rank] at different pay rates. Your question is military-specific and the military rank structure isn't exactly the most efficient or practical in many cases.

Maybe, and this is just an observation, if you spent more time doing work instead of asking hypothetical questions, which in turn can take hours to answer, you wouldn't be at work till 9:00 p.m. Just speaking hypothetically. LOL

Medals and points are cute, but let's be real. Pay me.

Root cause; eight equitable tasks don't exist for the eight folks.
You still have to reward the hard worker and weed out the weak.
We are human.

Whoever has their green Skype messenger light on the longest
each day should get more pay.

Your best guy/gal always gets somewhat punished. He gets
more work assigned to him because the boss knows it will get
done faster and done better. As a chief, I was as guilty of this as
anyone. Shouldn't have done it, but I did it nonetheless. I did,
however, reward my hard chargers with solid EPRs, medals, and
schools over the average or poor performers. So hard to put out
a poor performer these days.

In my opinion is that everyone has a boss. If their boss stated their expectations based on the goals of the organization up-front and gave honest feedback (hard to do sometimes but necessary), then those who achieve will pass up those who just show up to collect a paycheck. Unfortunately, people make excuses for why others can't achieve and lose sight of the fact that not everyone is an achiever. Likewise, some people are never meant to promote past a certain level.

Seniority coupled with continued work performance can't be beat. It's when seniority evolves into a feeling of "I deserve this or that because I've been here forever" that the grapes start to sour.

In a perfect world, every boss would do their job at the top and expect nothing short of greatness. Unfortunately, the world in which we now live is more about hugs and not hurting feelings. This ultimately hinders the organization and moves us further away from doing the simplest thing, namely, our job.

So, simply put, no, all eight won't ever contribute equally. They are paid the same because their bosses make excuses for them along the way and give them a hug and a chance to promote. Seniority deserves more pay, but only if the bosses (because everyone has one) continue to provide guidance and feedback on how they are doing. Attendance-based compensation isn't acceptable, but it's the world we live in. I don't know what the simple fix is, only that there isn't one. Over time culture changes from the top will start to evolve the organization and change it to a performance-based compensation system.

My two cents: This applies to all organizations and not just the military.

Leading Across, Leading Up

> *"One who has never learned to follow can never lead."*
> — Aristotle

I find it interesting when people make excuses as to why they don't feel they can influence the things that happen within their organization. There are so many myths about leadership and influence, and it's important you backhand those excuses and begin earning the credibility needed to influence daily operations, interactions, and even policy.

An upsetting truth is that too often people in the military talk to a person's rank rather than their intellect. It's as if they are staring at your stripes when you speak, filtering what they want to hear and developing their own opinions midsentence. What a shame. But with credibility and a touch of courage, you can change this perspective and people will start taking you at your word.

Have you ever seen an organization where the lowest person on the totem pole has too much influence? I know I have. Ever sees a secretary, who works directly for the boss, influence the boss? Happens all the time. You, too, can position yourself to influence the top of your organization.

If you're reading this book, you're likely in middle management. You are the backbone of the system, the one who has to survive the ongoing pressures from above, below, and all around. Middle management is where the rubber hits the road, where organizations either thrive or fail. It's no wonder the majority of people who buy self-development books are somewhere in the middle, where the pursuit of growth still burns strong and the desire to lead begins to gain traction. For these reasons, I put together a section on being in the middle and how you can debunk the notion that you have to be at the top to be a strong influence on the organization, all the way up to the boss.

Here a few things to note to get to where you can put a tidbit in the boss's ear and influence the entire work center. Unapologetically, I've taken notable pieces from John C. Maxwell's *The 360° Leader: Developing Your Influence from Anywhere in the Organization* (2005).

Maxwell believes that leaders who are deficit in leadership skills are hoarders of information. They protect their work from everyone to ensure they receive full credit when the work is completed. He mentions several times that true leaders share everything. They share their greatest ideas, their invested projects, and their hardest work. It is those who will reap the most benefits and, like cream, rise to the top. Sounds amazing, right? I work to hold on to this premise, despite the countless times I've seen the hard work of one person be claimed by another. A bullet drafted on a package by someone who wasn't even present during the process they are noting. The only way to combat this is to be a leader of courage and speak up. Even though we see this stuff happening in our Air Force, I know that what Maxwell says here is the mecca of leadership, and if we individually work on being this type of leader, we can slowly erode the wall of bullshit that others are trying to build.

According to Maxwell, there are three key concepts about leading up and leading across. (His third concept—leading down—is where you directly influence a subordinate's growth.)

1. **Leading Up**: This means you lighten your leader's load by doing everything others won't do. You know when to be aggressive and make a stand for what you believe in.

2. **Leading Across**: The person who helps others achieve their goals within their peer group will be the same one who others go to for advice. If you are moving forward and then look back and find others following behind you, you are leading. If you don't, you're merely taking a walk.

3. **Leading Down**: Helping others below you reach their full potential is something they will remember forever. Leading down means you only look down to others when you are reaching down to help them up.

Books to Change Your Life

> *"If we encounter a man of rare intellect,*
> *we should ask him what books he reads."*
> — Ralph Waldo Emerson

The military is a stressful job. A 2015 study by CareerCast has us active-duty folks ranked as number two in the nation for the most stressful job (firefighter is number one). After searching the topic I realized all the polls had "enlisted military member" in the top three. This validation of what all of us in the military already know made me think of all the ways we can try to reduce that stress level. Of course, we can help relieve stress by listening to music, exercising, even drinking tea, but reading will really help you refrain from posting a "Bang your head here" sign on your office wall.

Stress /noun/: *The confusion created when one's mind overrides their natural instinct to slap the ever-loving shit out of a person who clearly deserves it.*

Aside from being an awesome stress reliever, reading makes you smarter and is the ultimate development tool. Here are a few other reasons why reading is so important:

1. Like I said, reading makes you smarter.

2. Reading develops your vocabulary (if you say f—k too much, it's because you lack sufficient adjectives in your vocabulary).

3. Reading improves your concentration in a world that pulls you in too many directions.

4. Reading enhances your imagination.

5. Reading makes you interesting.

6. Reading improves your memory by allowing for comprehension and insight.

The reasons to read are not limited to the ones mentioned above, and everyone has their own reasons as to why reading helps you.

The single most important thing I try to do when briefing the younger generation is to bring a stack of my favorite books. It is so encouraging when I see people writing down book titles as I do show-and-tell with my ever-changing collection. Although I have many bookshelves overflowing with knowledge at the house, there are 11 books I honestly believe everyone should read to improve themselves personally and professionally. I didn't pick these books, but rather mentors, coaches, friends, and family recommended them. Each has a little something different to offer, but I believe these are perfect for the military member wanting to truly develop.

Brian Tracy, *Eat That Frog! 21 Great Ways to Stop Procrastinating and Get More Done in Less Time* (2001)

Mark Twain said that if the first thing you do each day is eat a live frog, you can go through the day knowing that is probably the worst thing that is going to happen to you that day.

This is the message Brian Tracy uses as he explains how procrastination is a cancer to success. Confusing activity with accomplishment is something most people do because they fail to resist the temptation to finish the small things first. Tracy explains that if you have a list of things to do, 20 percent of them will account for 80 percent of actual, tangible productivity. This book is one of my most valuable books because I'm constantly trying to get a million things done every day. Reminding myself to eat the frog and knock out the hardest, ugliest task or project first has provided opportunities for me to succeed and feel true satisfaction upon completion.

Timothy Ferriss, *The 4-Hour Workweek: Escape 9–5, Live Anywhere, and Join the New Rich* (2007)

Want to learn how to out-source things in your life, increase productivity by decreasing actual work, or even automate your life? Well, this book has all that and more. I read this book during a long flight over the Atlantic, and the two things I took from it and apply to this day are outsourcing projects (hiring a virtual assistant to handle menial tasks) and minimizing my email time to just two hours a day. In addition, Ferriss argues that we should be on a low-information diet and we must all learn to say no. This book is just cool. If nothing else, Ferriss motivates you to liberate yourself from the day-to-day grind and live your life!

John C. Maxwell, *The 21 Irrefutable Laws of Leadership: Follow Them and People Will Follow You* (1998)

If you asked Kaleth Wright, the Chief Master Sergeant of the Air Force, what his favorite book is, he would refer you to this gem. Why? Because the laws apply to everyone who aspires to lead others, whether in the service or not. Maxwell uses deliberate and easy-to-follow laws. After I read this book, I realized where my strengths lay and where my personal growth needs enhancement. The biggest takeaway from the book was the perfectly penned quote "Leadership is influence—nothing more, nothing less." Like the Chief Wright, I highly recommend that everyone explore this book. It is perfect for writing notes, highlighting, and planting the seeds to effectively grow.

Viktor E. Frankl, *Man's Search for Meaning: An Introduction to Logotherapy* (1963)

When you complain about your environment, always remember things could be worse. The turbulence in your life, the things you take for granted, others are praying for. I hold onto this sentence after reading this disturbing memoir about life in a World War II concentration camp. Frankl was the director of therapy at a mental hospital in Vienna before the war. He was incarcerated by the Nazis and decided to observe and write a mental, emotional, and physical account of the most appalling time in history. For Frankl, the situation confirmed Friedrich Nietzsche's words, "He who has a why to live for can bear with almost any how." On a smaller scale, we all are trying to position ourselves in our own environments and need to pause every now and then and ask ourselves what our purpose is.

Rhonda Byrne, *The Secret* (2006)

Do your thoughts become things? Is there a law of attraction in this universe where *like* attracts *like*? Byrne and many experts believe so. The premise here is that your thoughts send out a frequency to the universe and the universe responds to that frequency by bringing you more of the same. For example, if you *think* you have bad luck, you will. The cool thing is the opposite is also true.

I read this book while waiting for a flight to Okinawa, and I believe the basic principle. Its message is similar to what CMSgt Ramon Colon-Lopez says to his team: "If you want to soar with eagles, don't hang around with turkeys." If you emit a frequency to the universe that you are a person of high worth, integrity, and positive energy, you will receive that back into your life. Cool, right?

Paulo Coelho, *The Alchemist* (1998)

This is the only novel in the stack because, to be honest, I don't really read that many novels. *The Alchemist* is a rare exception because it is about the pursuit of happiness, something we all want and desire. A young shepherd wants to find hidden treasures in Egypt, but to do so he has to leave his comfort zone and overcome his fears. Along the way are many obstacles, often unbearable, but the shepherd realizes that, despite any obstacle, one cannot lose sight of his "personal legend," that is, your own definition of happiness. This book opened my mind to dreaming big and not being afraid of failure. There are several lessons to be learned by reading this masterpiece.

Stephen R. Covey, *The Seven Habits of Highly Effective People: Restoring the Character Ethic* (1989)

If any one book opened up my mind to developing through reading, it is this one. In fact, I'm going to break down these habits so you can immediately take something away from this:

1. **Be Proactive**: My alarm clock on my iPhone flashes this every morning as a reminder that the world will not wait for me, so I better move forward.

2. **Begin with the End in Mind**: Anthony Robbins said, "You can't plan for your day if you haven't planned for your life."

3. **Put First Things First**: Be sure to manage yourself. Your activities should aim for the second habit.

4. **Think Win/Win**: I love this one. Genuine feelings for mutually beneficial situations.

5. **Seek First to Understand, Then Be Understood**: When you genuinely listen to people, they will reciprocate. This allows influence to flourish.

6. **Synergize**: Combine the strengths of others, or in other words: *Teamwork* makes the dream work.

7. **Sharpen the Saw**: Reading anything and everything that pertains to your personal goals or career field allows the mental cultivation you need to rise.

Dale Carnegie, *How to Win Friends and Influence People* (1936)

What do you naturally do when you see a smiling baby? You smile back! Smiling is contagious.

This is just one of 30 principles Carnegie discusses in detail for your absorbing pleasure. Other principles that caught my attention and are applicable to us in the military are, well, the other 29! To be honest, if there is one book you should read (with the exception to My Rich Uncle of course), it should be this one. It is written in a way that invites you to learn what it takes to influence others while being genuine. My main takeaway is that people love to talk about themselves. We are a narcissistic society, and if you can get people to talk about themselves, they tend to enjoy the conversation. That leads to my favorite Carnegie quote: "The world is full of people who are grabbing and self-seeking. So the rare individual who unselfishly tries to serve others has an enormous advantage. He has little competition."

Alfred Lansing, *Endurance: Shackleton's Incredible Voyage* (1959)

In 1914 Sir Ernest Shackleton led 27 men on the ship *Endurance*. By December the ship was stuck in ice and drifted for months. But the failed expedition is not the important thing; this is a book about survival. Lansing writes a mind-boggling account of Shackleton's expedition, detailing the struggle to survive. He vividly depicts the harsh winter in the coldest place on earth, but ultimately he poignantly describes the nobility of these men and their indefatigable will to live.

This book is on my list because it's a straight-up catalog of misery that trumps any mediocre strife we may encounter in our day-to-day lives. Don't think so? *They had to wipe their butts with ice!*

Now that's bad.

John C. Maxwell, *The 360° Leader* (2005)

This is the second book on the list by Maxwell. You know why? Because I feel his straightforward and smooth execution of deliberate development is exactly what we need to retain his important messages. He offers solutions to a problem we all face in our organizations: the frustration of not being in the top spot and therefore not being able to have influence across the board. Maxwell, however, does an excellent job explaining why we can make significant, influential contributions, regardless of our rank. This book is perfect for enlisted members! My main takeaway is the section that has you ponder why the secretary of the organization has so much influence over the boss.

This is proof you can positively influence the momentum, regardless of your pay grade.

Steven Pressfield, *The War of Art: Break Through the Blocks and Win Your Inner Creative Battles* (2002)

This is the stone-cold stunner of motivational books. Pressfield describes how resistance is the real monster within us all. Only those who can find their muse and destroy resistance can really make a dent in their life. Do you want your legacy to be like sticking your hand in a bucket of water, pulling it out, and realizing you didn't make a difference? I don't think so. You are better than that. We are all better than that. Pressfield points out that we all have unique talents and strengths and must overcome resistance to bring them to the surface. I swear, every time I open this book, within 10 minutes I'm pacing the floor and asking why I let procrastination kick my ass all the time. This is a must-read.

Books are super cool. I know I'm in the minority here, but a real book is where it's at. I can't do the Kindle thing very well. It just doesn't feel real. I need that book smell. That feeling that you're holding something powerful in your hand, something enlightening. I can't go for long without reading and neither should you. Be like Warren Buffet and read! read! read!

Go ahead, turn the page, you know you want to.

From the Horse's Mouth

> *"Judge a man by his questions rather than his answers."*
> — Pierre-Marc-Gaston de Lévis

This section is really fascinating because I had an opportunity to speak with some of the top enlisted leaders as well as take some valuable nuggets of wisdom from military leaders around the world. It's no secret you cannot truly be successful all by yourself. It is imperative that we constantly read and listen to those above us who have made it to the pinnacle. Why on earth would you join the military, climb up this corporate ladder, only to stop on a middle rung? As John C. Maxwell pointed out, we all have a lid. This lid is up to us, and only through deliberate development can we continue to climb the ladder. One key decision to make is the decision to reach out to those above us and ask questions that will get you to lift your leg and reach for the next rung up.

The following fragmented goodness is from multiple leaders who I feel have assisted me in my journey. I may not be a chief, but my mind is always on the move, and my climbing will never cease. I fail all the time and these people collectively lift me up and keep me on my path. Use these at your choosing. When you need a lift, flip through the pages and find yourself one-on-one with one of these titans of leadership. Enjoy!

General Colin Powell is a Badass

It can be daunting to try to write an effective chapter on leadership when I have so much to learn myself. The last thing I want to do is feed you a bunch of crap. It would be like a twenty-something manager, clipboard in hand and a smirk on his face, walking up to a sixty-something employee and offering some life lessons. The sixty-something would listen, but I assure you he has an internal smirk of his own.

The thing is, leadership, like life lessons, comes with time. Lots of time. We are supposed to believe we are leaders in the military because we find ourselves quickly in charge of many people or we sign an appointment letter making us responsible for $2M worth of dusty equipment. Hopefully, our heads don't blow up so we can't climb out of our ego trip. Real leadership, however, comes from a constant and deliberate desire to learn and develop every day. During that process, we learn nuggets of information that can be thrown into our cache of leadership knowledge. That cache will grow over time, and lucky for me, I have some pretty cool stuff in that cache now. Notably, some of those leadership lessons came from Gen. Colin Powell, a legend in his own right. If you don't know who he is, that sucks. He was a well-known general and full-time badass. I also think he was the best National Security Advisor ever. Because we, too, are in the service, it would make sense to perk up our ears and hear what this guy has to say.

Here are some takeaways from General Powell for that cache of yours:

- *"Being responsible sometimes means pissing people off."*

  This goes back to that horrible thing we have going on where everyone gets a first-place trophy just for showing up. This is wrong and leads to organizational mediocrity. Trying to get everyone to like you simply isn't going to happen, so you must be honorable in your decisions, no matter how they are received. If you fail to differentiate between the go-to player and the bottom-feeders, you will only upset those who work the hardest.

- *"The day your people stop coming to you with their problems is the day you have stopped leading them."*

What else needs to be said? At that point, they have either lost confidence in you or they don't trust you.

- *"Leadership does not emerge from blind obedience."*

Too often we are so black-and-white in the military. "Well, the AFI [Air Force instruction] says this." Who cares? Sometimes we need to challenge even the pros we observe and are mentored by. We can all agree that when policy comes from the brass, it often has adverse effects on those of us working.

- *"You don't know what you can get away with until you try."*
Leaders need to know when to ask for forgiveness versus asking for permission. A good example is this book. It isn't your run-of-the-mill military book. I knew I wanted to provide everyone with some real talk, so I'm going for it without permission. Well, with the exception of the legal stuff that would get me in jail.

I love these lessons and go back to them often. They are so against the grain. Funny, many things we are told that are considered socially acceptable are often the things that get you nowhere. Sometimes we need to listen to guys like General Powell. I mean, the guy used to take off his uniform during meetings to ensure open dialogue. What a bad ass.

How to Be a Command Chief, Featuring CMSgt Edwin Ludwigsen

Why stand on a ladder and not climb to the top? The 1 percent at the top of our ladder are the chiefs around us. Of that 1 percent, some go on to other forms of chiefs, notably, command chiefs. This is the leader who acts as a true advocate for us at the installation level and works directly for the wing commander himself. This is one helluva job and takes a certain type of person. But what is the secret? Is there a secret? The current command chief at Spangdahlem AB, Germany, is a guy who made it rather quickly to this level. There is a magnetism about him that makes people want to listen when he speaks. For these and other reasons, I asked him a few questions that you might want to know when it comes to how one achieves that position and prepare yourself for what would surely be a challenging job.

Chief, you are a young *command chief*. How did you make it to this level so quickly?

> Some may consider me a young command chief, but I've never looked at age as a discriminator for leadership potential. It really is an honor to be considered for command chief duty. As for how I made it to this level so quickly, I like to think it is based on my character, experience, and demonstrated leadership over the course of my Air Force career. Additionally, there is no way I'm where I am today without some very good mentors, great supervisors, a supportive family, and quite frankly good timing.

What is one thing you feel you did right when you were a middle manager?

> I did not worry about things beyond my control. As a supervisor [middle manager] my focus was always on taking care of my people and getting the job done. I noticed very early in my career that some peers would complain about things they could not control, and that seemed to have negative impact on their work ethic. I chose to look at the positive side of things and wait for the appropriate time and place to offer feedback on the issues that bothered me or that I liked to see changed.

What are the methods, methodology, mind-set, and motivation that got you to where you are today?

> Quite simple, be yourself. Always do your best. And treat others like you want to be treated.

How does a *chief get selected to be a command chief?*

> By their boss! There is a deliberate process managed by the
> Chiefs' Group and MAJCOM command chiefs for hiring
> command chiefs, but ultimately it comes down to the wing CC (or
> higher level) matching the chief to the needs of his or her wing.
> The only role I played in the process was as a candidate.

In hindsight, what is one thing you wish you did differently in your career?

> That's not an easy question because I think I've had a pretty
> amazing ride up to this point. I often wish I had the opportunity to
> serve as a first sergeant though.
> It seems every chief has a go-to acronym or saying *about*
> leadership. What's yours?

I honed my three Es with a supervisor, and they are my basic expectation for my airmen: Energy, Effort, Expertise.

The Truth About Getting Promoted, 18th Chief Master Sergeant of the Air Force, CMSgt Kaleth Wright

Most people know Chief Wright as Coach, and he's one of the most influential leaders I've ever had the pleasure to know. My first encounter with him was long before where he is now, at the pinnacle of the enlisted force; it was on the baseline of a basketball court in Okinawa, Japan. The first words I ever heard him say were a loud and deliberate "Go!" as we all ran another suicide (conditioning regimen in basketball) for missing a free throw. Coach used his off-time to develop us into warriors on and off the court. Aside from being a chief in the dental squadron, where the demand was extremely high for his knowledge and skills, he ensured we were well-oiled machines. Admittedly, I wasn't one of the best players on the team, but Coach still took his time to leverage the strengths of each and every one of us.

Fast-forward a few tours and countries later, playing catch-up through social media, I had the privilege of running into Coach at my SNCO induction ceremony. Unlike almost every other leader at that level, he immediately asked specific questions about my life, those I am close with, and specifics about my professional growth. He was the USAFE-AFAFRICA command chief at the time, meeting thousands of people up and down the hierarchy, and he remembered my life specifics. This was incredible to me. I have a hard time remembering the names of people I see all the time, let alone someone I knew long ago. Keep in mind, I'm not nearly as in demand as Chief Wright. This is the kind of guy he is. He's personable and approachable. Chief Wright was the right (no pun intended) selection for our top boss.

Something I've noticed to be true about those who have had huge successes in life and career is that they have a magnetism about them. People want to be around them. This magnetism for people acts as a catalyst, propelling them to the top. This is true when I speak of Chief Wright and the success he has had during his decorated career.

As I thought about who I should interview for this section, I asked, Who would be able to really talk about the methods, motivation, and mind-sets it takes to get promoted and sustain potential during a career? As if it was meant to happen, Chief Wright, just before taking the helm as the top chief, sent out a short article titled "The Truth About Getting Promoted." Perfect timing! What follows is my best attempt at extrapolating the nut of this article.

- Chief Wright recommended studying no earlier than four months prior to your test date. He said the most important aspect of this foundation is to let your family and spouse know that those four months will be full of studying and quiet time.

- He said he does most of his studying in the library and has found this to be very effective.

- Whatever you decide your study times are, never deviate from them!

- Never study more than one hour at a time.

- Forget about calculators that show you what you need to score and *always* shoot for 100 percent. This is a mental thing that cannot be undone.

- Inventory your study material and develop a schedule based on three hours of study time per day for four months.

- Alternate studying your PDG (the professional development guide) two days and your SKT (specialty knowledge test) three days. Don't study all of one for a month or so and then work on the other. Chances are you will do much better on the one you most recently studied.
- Don't take more than two days per chapter of the PDG.
- Use the weekend as flex days. They can be used to tie up loose ends.
- There are four phases for effective studying:
  - Read and highlight each chapter to your heart's content
  - Annotate (write down bullets of important information)
  - Review (read through all your highlights and bullets)
  - Validate (use web-based programs only after the previous studying has been completed)

The fact that Chief Wright shared his secrets is awesome. Growing up in the Air Force, it seems everyone wants to find a secret recipe for promotion. The truth is, I don't think there is a mysterious concoction, but if there were, CMSAF Wright and his points to remember are probably less than a tablespoon of salt away from fool-proof. So what are you waiting for? Are you approaching four months prior to your test date? You better get on it before Chief Wright puts your ass on the baseline for some more cardio training!

Getting Fired Up, Command Chief (ret.) Juan Lewis

Chief! Why the hell are you always so fired up?

You got to do what you love and love what you do. I loved wearing the uniform. I love the Air Force and all the opportunities it offers. The Air Force instilled pride, enthusiasm, and passion inside me that inspired me to take care of the heroes. Just the idea to give back to the Air Force and the heroes keeps my PEP level running high.

What do the younger generation need to be doing to be successful in today's Air Force?

> I'm proud of the younger generation for joining the Air Force. If I can offer them some tips, they are to control the controllable and follow the ABCs. First, they must always have the right attitude, regardless of the challenge and situation. Their attitude has the ability to turn bad to good, good to great, and great to outstanding. Next, they must expand the foundation they learned in basic training. Finally, they need to continue to challenge themselves to be better than yesterday but less than tomorrow.

As the former *command chief* of AETC (*Air Education and Training Command*), what is one thing you think we are doing great when it comes to training our folks?

> The Air Force is providing fundamental training opportunities. The in-residence PME (professional military education) has expanded on the years, providing heroes more tools to serve in a greater capacity. Job proficiency classes have increased too. Heroes have some incredible venues to perfect their craft as true professionals.

I *know* you always keep it real, *so* what is something the Air Force must fix or be doomed?

> Taking care of people. It's not what you say, it's not what you do, it's all about how the heroes feel. I believe as a whole, the Air Force could do a much job of taking care of its heroes. In addition, the Air Force must restore the pride and return to its heritage. For example, when was the last time a wing hosted a formal dining-out ceremony? Most of these formal military ceremonies are modified to deplete formalities.

What is a misconception out there that people think is true?

> There are several misconceptions. One of the first is that everyone is a wingman. There are so many folks who do not have a wingman. Also, when troubled heroes need help, it appears their wingmen disappear. The other big misconception

is that leaders are taking care of the heroes. In most cases, taking care of the troops is a bumper-sticker slogan and not a reality.

Your Attitude and Your Altitude

> *"The Pessimist sees difficulty in every opportunity.*
> *The Optimist sees opportunity in every difficulty."*
> — Winston Churchill

How can we remain optimistic in any situation? I try to remind myself I am the only one in control of my emotions and actions. Life, as they say, is 20 percent what happens to you and 80 percent how you react.

So how can we remain optimistic in the tough times? Is there really opportunity in every difficult situation? Death? Divorce? Unemployment? It's easy to feel overwhelmed and fall into a depressed, pessimistic state of mind. But you are always in control. No one else. Just you.

Here are three ways to gain control when times are tough:

1. Look for something positive. Let's say you just got moved to a different work schedule that minimizes your time with your family. This sucks but the time shift will surely open doors to get things done you couldn't do otherwise. Remember that positivity is a *choice*.

2. Remove negative things in your life. The easiest way to seek optimism is to remove the negative factors you can control. Blaming outside influences will get you nowhere fast.

3. When something negative happens, force yourself to think about the situation. Often it's easy to see the bad; it's a natural tendency to be negative as humans. Only when we think critically about it can we find something positive. You will surprise yourself as you discover many positive things from something that had an immediate negative reaction.

Optimism is contagious. Don't ever forget that like attracts like. Your positive energy will flow to everyone around you. In the end, pessimism leads to weakness, but optimism is the path to power.

How to Not Let Others Bring You Down

Some people don't like you, and there's nothing you can do about it. In fact, you are being judged right now. Although this is true, thankfully, most people don't even care you're alive. Trust me, that is a good thing! Knowing this fundamental truth will free you from wasting time trying to be liked and allow you to move forward and focus on what is truly important. The key is: *Don't give a damn.*

Here's some more essential information for you. When someone doesn't like you, nothing happens. Haters are going to hate. That's their job! Stop trying to take away their job! Instead, focus on the people who matter. Those are the people closest to you. Whether it be your spouse, friends, family, these people are your legitimate advocates and deserve your time. I read an essay by Julien Smith titled *"The Complete Guide to Not Giving a Fuck,"* and he went into detail about how we are always trying to impress new people who actually don't matter. He hits the nail on the head when he explains that we take those who matter for granted and impress someone else until we end up taking them for granted and continue this horrible cycle. The point is this, Focus on the true champions around you and stop giving a shit about the haters. Get yourself out of that prison, you know, the one where you are always trying to please others. As Smith brilliantly concludes, "It doesn't fucking matter."

Okay, so that was pretty abrasive. But life is abrasive and life is short, so do yourself a favor and don't worry too much about those around you because they either like you or they don't. Either way, you should be magnanimous and worry about those people who actually impact your life.

There have been many times when I see someone doing something that seems like they are being placed in a more important function than you or that they are being favored by leadership. Those are the times you need to worry only about yourself and those you can positively affect the most.

Okay, I'm done. Let's move on.

Stop the Stupid: AF CPI

> *"We don't have to be a rocket scientist to be innovative,*
> *we just need to Stop the Stupid."*
> — Lynette Wright

What in the hell is CPI? Continuous process improvement, pervasively known as AFSO21 (Air Force Smart Operations for the 21st Century). CPI is gold. Shit, it's platinum. This is the most important thing you can be a part of in the Air Force because it is a skill set that, if acquired, will set you up in spectacular fashion when you transition out. If you want to shine, if you want to lead, if you want to be promoted, get on this train.

Without putting you to sleep, I briefly describe what CPI is and how you can become what we call a CPI Ninja. In short, CPI is all about taking out the non-value-added activities that plague our everyday process. Focusing on the customer, we lead teams to map the process, establish flow, implement tools, and eliminate waste. This is the art of lean thinking, and it will forever change the way you look at things.

Waste is everywhere. In the Air Force, we see it in the form of waiting. "Hurry up and wait" is its purest form in every transactional process around us and it needs to stop. It is just plain stupid. Waste can be seen in many forms, so let me throw another acronym at you, TIMWOOD.

Transportation: Any time material or product is moving around, it is waste. I love the example of the folks at one base loading up a truck twice a week and driving it over an hour to another installation so work can be done. Even if we feel this is a necessity, it is still waste.

Inventory: We should be on the ultimate episode of Hoarders. We always accumulate, and in a business (which we are), this is waste. It costs money to store stuff and the old "maybe I will need this one day" stage has to be eliminated along with all those extra D batteries. Did you know the Air Force has $54M in C-130 parts that don't fit the new C-130J model? Why do you think we reduced the number of printers? The inventory of those toner cartridges was costing us millions.

Motion: Take a look at a process and then map a sketch of the layout. Using a marker, draw where the people go within it. You will end up with a map that looks like a bowl of spaghetti. This is motion waste. It is the same as transportation, except it is simply a person, not a person with a product. Know any examples?

Waiting: Not much needs to be said about this one. Waiting is everywhere and it is a waste. Check out the AMC Passenger Travel story below.

Overproduction: When you produce too much of anything, it is waste. If you build 1,000 of something and only sell 620, you are going to lose.

Overprocessing: Routing slips! This is a classic form of overprocessing and it wastes people's time. Overprocessing anything is a form of waste. Another example is needing multiple approval signatures just to get something simple done (think DTS [Defense Travel System]). Stop the stupid already.

Defects: When you don't do something right the first time, you have to go back and correct it. This is precisely why you should build standard work into your unit's processes.

Examples and opportunities are everywhere in the military. We just kind of get by day to day, spending money, wasting people's time, going home, and drinking a beer. I mean, it isn't *my* money after all, right? It is money the taxpayers give up with the expectation that we use it correctly and efficiently.

CPI is still, to this day, an untapped resource. Not enough people are getting involved. This is *exactly* why you should. How do you get involved? Simply find out if your wing has an innovation and transformation office (ITO). They will be hosting basic-level courses to include the sought after green-belt course (see why it's called CPI Ninja?). If you become green-belt certified, not only do you receive a special experience identifier (SEI), but you also get invited to change things that affect the entire base. Here are just a couple of positive changes I was able to implement with our awesome CPI teams from 2015 to 2017:

- Reduced wait time in the vehicle registration office 30 percent.

- Built an all-new housing website and reduced customers' trips to the office from eight to two.
- Saved $648K in PPE (personal protective equipment) by simply not listening to the ridiculous policy's bench stock quota.
- Conducted a base-wide audit of 115 facilities, divesting 50K square feet of space.
- Built an all-new digital business platform for AFSC. It's now used across the enterprise for daily needs.
- Standardized AF vehicle training. New lesson plans were disseminated around the globe.

To get those monkeys in your brains working, here is an example of why we need CPI and probably something you can relate to as well.

AMC Passenger Travel

There I was, sitting in my room at Incirlik AB, Turkey. I was teamed with a colleague from the MAJCOM (Major Command Air Force) to teach Green Belt 2.0 for the week at the request of the wing command chief. It was about time to head over to the passenger terminal and check in for the flight the next morning.

The day prior, I had called on the hour, every hour and, depending on who I spoke with, received conflicting information. I knew something was messed up! When I arrived at the counter, I handed the service representative my ID and orders. He said we needed to come back for a show time of 0330 for the 0730 flight. Keep in mind, this was the *only* flight out that morning and yet we had to be there four hours early?

As the customer, I asked, "Why is it necessary to be so early?"

The representative used the old "It's always been that way," and then he was interrupted by the master sergeant behind him. He stepped up, full of confidence, and blurted the one thing I can't stand the most. He looked me in the eyes and said, "Because our regulation says so."

I expected this. "Which regulation is this," I asked. "Are we talking about 24-101?"

He said yes. I pulled out my laptop, hit up the Wi-Fi, and looked up the regulation right there. I found this master sergeant, who was in charge and had been doing this for who knows how long, was incorrect. Plain as day, the regulation stated for Space-R passengers to arrive two hours and 20 minutes prior to departure time.

Now, the person in charge, a young captain, came up and joined this intriguing discussion. He said they didn't "feel" they could get all the passengers through in that time. That it's always been three and half to four hours prior.

The next morning, we collected some data on this process:

- Bags through security: 5 minutes
- Check-in with bag drop: 5 minutes
- Sit and wait: 2 hours 37 minutes
- Go through passport control: 30 minutes
- Sit and wait: 1 hour 23 minutes
- Head to plane: 10 minutes

Notice all that is over the time allotted? That's because the 0730 flight didn't board until well after departure time. Does this process sound familiar? But at the end of the day, who cares about you anyway? You are just the customer, and everyone is on a salary, so no one cares. You see, that's the problem! We're accustomed to substandard performance, so we're used to being treated like cattle and not customers. We just go with the flow—or the lack thereof.

As a CPI Ninja, you can be the one who puts a stop to this nightmare. You can charter an event and make a tangible difference that affects innumerable people. This is an opportunity that will not only help others, but I guarantee will continue to set you apart.

I believe in CPI so much that if you are reading and want to truly be a part of this paradigm shift, contact me at andrewkehl@hotmail.com (yes, hotmail), and I will get your name to the right person on your base so you can attend the next CPI offering.

It's that important!

Chapter 9

Military Intelligence (and Other Oxymorons)

BLUF and Other Funny AF Things

Between quarterly packages and EPRs, we all have those words that are ridiculous. Spearheaded comes to mind as a word used *way* too much along with the well-known (and well-played-out) tip of the spear.

It isn't just EPRs and packages, we as an Air Force created our own language, and I'm pretty sure we find ourselves overusing it! Let's be honest, the more you're in the military, the more these new and often silly words are used. In a feeble attempt to bring a little humor to My Rich Uncle, here are some pretty funny sayings and jargon we use make me crack a smile.

Airman with a capital A
alcon
at the end of the day
bleeding edge
buy-in
can-do attitude
caveat
comprehensive
dfac
<u>fit to fight</u>
footstomp

it is what it is
let's touch base
<u>leverage</u>
low-hanging fruit
piggyback
rog (instead of roger)
synergy/synergize
tracking
vector
volun-told and mandatory fun (it isn't exactly volunteering if you're told)
whole-person concept"

All of those are pretty funny and unique to us, but the silliest one was learned in PME (professional military education): tactical breathing, that is, the ability to control your breathing in times when you most need to breathe efficiently. I love it!

What Is Up with BLUF?

I received a BLUF (bottom line upfront) email with nothing but the BLUF line. I don't think they knew what they were doing. If you want to get the bottom line upfront, then put the bottom line in the email subject line. If you're trying to be as efficient as you can with your written communication, then the email subject should include enough information so the recipient understands what the message is about.

Hats

The first thing I would do if the Air Force ever screws up and makes me the boss is to get rid of hats. What purpose do they serve? At some point, leaders should ask themselves why the hell we still wear them. Is it tradition? Is it for those rare times we are in formation? Who knows? All I know is they jack up my hair, get thrown onto tables, and are misplaced more often than I misplace my car keys. Hats simply don't make much sense, and how many people would actually fight to save the hats if a policy announced they were no longer required? Probably not many.

Fire! Ready . . . Aim . . .

Recently, the Air Force pushed out a new form of correspondence PME (professional military education). We know it as Courses 14 and 15. They are prerequisites to attend the in-residence course for NCO and SNCO progression. Basically, you have no choice but to do them. Without them, you can pretty much rest assured you will not progress any further. Those ABUs (airman battle uniforms) will fade to white because the stripes will be there longer than those D batteries in the office drawer you said I might need one day.

Course 15 was immediately a giant pain in the ass. Looking for gaps in their time, NCOs across the Air Force with more than seven years' time in service (TIS) needed to finish it within a year of enrolling (which you had to do ASAP). From memes to Hitler movie satires, the masses injected their opinion (seriously, look up Hitler Course 15 on YouTube). From my perspective, I could see some value in getting people prepared for in-residence, and the material covered isn't all that bad. But the Air Force put some harsh repercussions at the end of this thing. If you do not complete the coursework within the prescribed time period, you are ineligible to reenlist or promote. This is hardcore!

Some members took a proactive approach and finished it as soon as possible (see best approach). Remember, we cannot control some things or most things. We just need to knock them out in this case. But do you think that is what happened across the spectrum? Nope! In fact, when it came to the final month, a third of the NCOs across the enterprise had not completed it. Completion included going through the 800+ pages of reading material and taking two tests (Set A and Set B). As you might imagine, the education centers filled up quickly, and there was little or no availability for the members to test. This I put squarely on the shoulders of the members. Hearing excuses like "I didn't have the time" is simply unacceptable. I know many of you will disagree with this notion, but if you cannot find the time to do the one thing that will actually keep you from making more money or even having a job, then you have to take a deep look at your priorities. Tip: Less Call of Duty, more Course 15.

Moving forward, members everywhere were scrambling to get waivers from their chain of command and drawing excuses from all over the place. Stress, already at an all-time high, was shooting through the roof. Like a volcano, steam became lava. This stress made its way to AFPC (Air Force Personnel Center, i.e., the people who implement all this stuff) and chaos ensued. Because there were so many people about to miss the deadline, the Air Force realized it couldn't accept such a loss. The shit got serious.

Fire! The Air Force placed stiff consequences on not completing Course 15 in time. The brass didn't understand the consequences if a significant portion of the whole didn't complete the requirement. So what happened? Did they say, "Hell, no, we won't redraw the line in the sand"? Did they stand firm so their people would understand actions have consequences? No. They extended the deadline six months, as if to say, "Dang it, for real this time, you better finish it!"

The point of this story is that we need to look at the things we do every day and realize we are doing a poor job of preparing prior to established deadlines. If you tell someone, "Get this done by COB Friday," make sure you have set up a realistic time line and provided the necessary resources for them to succeed. Understand that you need to hold the line, and if you don't, you will lose credibility. Just like when you coddle a screaming child, the NCOs will continue to scream when they want something. And do you know why? Because you—the Air Force—just made it very clear that you aren't very organized. I'm curious what will happen if everyone just doesn't do it in time again.

Reflective Belts

> "If I were a sniper, I would look at the folks on the base
> and aim just above the really shiny belt."
> — Robin Williams

Reflective belts are, in my opinion, useless. Here are a couple hilarious facts about them:

1. We used to be forced to wear them *with* our reflective PT gear! Now that is ultra-reflective stuff. It took a long time for the AF to remove that silly rule.
2. There are still many places, even in hostile environments, where reflective belts are mandatory! What!? Why would I want help a sniper find his target?
3. There is actually a Facebook page dedicated to these things. I'm serious. It's called I Hate Reflective Belts. Now, that's funny.
4. In a recent article about the crazy policy, Air Force officials said airmen can be admonished or face nonjudicial punishment for not wearing the belts when required.
5. The belt actually did come from a legitimate *need*. It started in the 1990s when leaders saw that many service members were jogging before dawn and after dusk, often on busy streets. So to prevent accidents, they had them wear the belt.

Okay, so now you are even more educated on what is most likely the most hated item in the military inventory. So get out there and fight the good fight, but don't forget your reflective belt!

What can I say? I had a lot of fun writing this book and I'm really grateful you took time out from your valuable time to read it.

The reality is that we really do have a wealthy relative in Uncle Sam, and as men and women who serve our country, we have a right to know about the ways we can maximize our time away from those we truly care about and, at times, venture into harm's way. Buried in the AFIs (Air Force instructions) are endless perks, we just need to look for them. Inside the minds and hearts of so many around us are even more perks in the form of wisdom and life lessons. Together, we can squeeze all the goodness that comes with being in this uniform. Sure, it can suck at times, and it's really easy to complain and moan about all the things we cannot control. But if you want to maximize your enlistment, stay away from your circle of concern and focus all your attention on your circle of influence. Make today a positive day and watch how fast the time goes by.

For those of you who I know personally and are reading this, thank you so much for being a part of my life and supporting this endeavor. Many of you have been rooting for me during the last two years of writing a sentence at a time, and I can't thank you enough. For those of you I don't know, please know we are all brothers and sisters in the Air Force. We may not have met, but if you ever need anything, reach out and I've got your back!

Thanks for reading *My Rich Uncle*. If you like it, please share your experience and like the blog on Facebook.

Who knows, there may be a sequel!

— A.J.

Index

About the Author

A.J. Kehl is a master sergeant (MSgt) in the U.S. Air Force. He began his career as a fire protection apprentice, graduating from the Louis F. Garland Fire Academy in the fall of 2003.

From there, he began a life-changing journey overseas stationed at Ramstein AB, Germany, where he quickly became a technical expert and taught emergency medical technician courses. Moving forward, A.J. found a home in sunny Las Vegas, Nevada, as a fire inspector. Not long thereafter, he was called to duty for deployment to Ali, Iraq. During his off time, he served as a VIP host at the world's largest nightclubs on the Las Vegas Strip.

Well aware that traveling was paramount to maximizing his time in the service, he set out for Okinawa, Japan, in late 2010, where he woke up daily to the glistening waters of the East China Sea. His time in Okinawa changed the trajectory of his career and earned him multiple Air Force medals, MAJCOM-level awards, and ultimately a quick promotion to technical sergeant. With a new outlook on his military career, A.J. flew across the world to a new station in Spangdahlem, Germany, where he leveraged his vast knowledge of the Air Force model and earned the installation's Sijan Award for Leadership. This culminated with his promotion to master sergeant on his first try, with only 11 years in service.

His knowledge of the Air Force and business led to a position working directly for the wing commander as the wing process manager for innovation and process improvement, where A.J. facilitated events that saved the wing over $29M and 245,000 man-hours and earn the Air Force's Innovator of the Year Award in 2016. A short time later, he became the Department of Defense Senior Fire Officer of the Year—the highest recognition in his career field.

A.J. continues to do everything he can to add value to his own and other people's lives. He earned a bachelor's in Fire Science, a master's in Organizational Leadership, and multiple graduate certificates in Leadership from Cornell University. He welcomes your questions or feedback: andrewkehl@hotmail.com.